SEEING
YOUR
VISION
COME  TRUE

by Paul Becker

This book is dedicated to my wife and co-worker in the Lord's vineyard, Cathy Becker.

She is my Gift from God. Cathy is my life partner and ministry partner. She helps me to see my visions from the Lord come true.

Contents

Dear Friend,

Here is a question for you to ask yourself:

"How can I help to establish
one million churches to reach the world for Christ?"

Like us, do you want to see the world won for Christ? At Dynamic Church Planting International, our hearts are bound together with a deep desire to see the people of the world become strong disciples of our Lord and Savior.

People in every nation of the world need Jesus. At DCPI, we believe the best way to help people find Jesus is to establish a dynamic, Christ-centered, bible teaching church in their midst. The best way get that job done is to equip the leaders of the church well.

That is our purpose at Dynamic Church Planting International: "Equipping leaders to plant dynamic churches worldwide" Church planters all around the world are crying out for good, high quality training.

Our DCPI Vision is to: "Equip leaders, churches and associations to impact the planting of one million dynamic churches to reach the world for Christ!

That's right! We see **one million churches planted**. We see great churches established in every one of the 238 nations of the world. We see a team of 5000 leaders who are actively training other leaders in the Biblical principles of church planting.

You can help! Wherever you live in the world, you can take part in the Million Church Vision.

You can pray for God to bring his Vision of a Million to fulfillment.

You can invest financially in the vision.

If you are a teacher or a leader, you can apply to join The Fellowship of the 5000. This is a team of DCPI Certified Trainers and Dynamic Associates who are bringing effective, high-quality church planting training to the nations of the world.

To learn more about participating in the Million Church Vision, go to DCPI's website: www.dcpi.org

Until the whole world knows Him!

Paul

Paul Becker
Founder and President
Dynamic Church Planting International

1

The Story of a Vision from God

The purpose of this book is to help Christians see their visions come true. I want to tell you a story about a vision that is coming true. Then, throughout the book, we will find the principles in the story that will help your vision come true.

In 1994 I was at a crossroads. I was 43 years old and confused. What was God's next step for my ministry?

For five years, I had served as the Director of Church Planting for a church growth ministry connected with Campus Crusade for Christ, and simultaneously as the Church Planting Director for a regional association of churches in Southern California. That second role was ending, and I needed God's wisdom. What did He want me to do next?

When I have big questions like this, I take a personal prayer retreat to inquire of God.

I drove to a favorite retreat site in the mountains east of San Diego, determined to spend my first day preparing to receive God's guidance. I repented of my sins, because to hear God you must have a repentant heart. I read the Word of God ravenously and submitted to His will. I spent time praising Him and thanking Him for His work in my life. I asked to join Him in what He was doing.

On the second day, I decided to take a favorite hike to the top of Stonewall Peak. When I hike in the mountains, I feel the joy of doing something God has made me to do. That day as I looked up at Stonewall Peak, its sheer rock summit shining in the sunlight, I smiled to myself.

I anticipated close communion with God during my walk. As I exerted my body, my spirit would connect with the Lord. I planned to jot down insights in a small notebook I carried in my pocket.

I prayed: "You know why I am here, my Lord. I have a major decision to make. What is my next ministry? Please communicate with me today, Lord. I am seeking your wisdom, your direction, your guidance for my future ministry. In the name of Jesus. Amen."

Then I began the hike. The spring air was warm and fragrant with pine needles, and I began to experience the joy of being with the Lord, hiking in His mountains.

Often I stopped to jot down my "consecrated thoughts," the result of having prepared my mind for godly reflections.

As I continued moving up the trail toward the peak, the Lord answered my question about the future: "Start a new non-profit ministry that is dedicated solely to equipping church planting leaders." I wrote it down. God's guidance had fulfilled the purpose for my prayer retreat.

By 1994 I had been taking prayer retreats for 18 years. I've learned that the Lord doesn't always answer the questions I'm asking. Sometimes He surprises me with answers to the questions I should have been asking! But over the years He has guided me in the major issues of my life, my family, and my ministry. This retreat was one of those times. He had directed me to begin a ministry solely devoted to equipping church planting. I was overcome with joy. Not just the joy of mountain climbing, but the joy of the Lord.

The next morning, I had breakfast with my dear friend and administrator, Jack Dempsey, in the small town near my retreat site. I shared my vision story with him, and he signed on as the first staff member of what became Dynamic Church Planting International. Shortly after that, we crafted our purpose statement: "Mentoring leaders to plant dynamic churches worldwide."

Next came our first vision statement, called the 20/20 Vision: Dynamic Church Planting International will impact the planting of 1000 churches by the year 2020.

Then we went to work on our values. What did we stand for? What was most important to us as we conducted the business of our mission? We began with six values:

1. Christ-centered, **Bible-teaching**: We work only with those church planting leaders who are Christ-centered and Bible-teaching.

2. **Compassion**: We have compassion for church planting leaders, their families, churches and associations.

3. Reproductive **Training**: We use materials and teaching techniques that trained mentors can reproduce.

4. **Cooperation**: We work to increase the effectiveness of churches, missions and associations in planting dynamic churches.

5. **Evangelism and Discipleship**: We strive to help plant churches that reach people for Christ and disciple them to maturity.

6. **Multiplication**: We seek to multiply the planting and establishing of churches with those whom we serve.

We recruited a Board of Directors and Dynamic Church Planting International (DCPI) was incorporated in 1995. In those early years, Jack and I had offices in my home.

We began to equip church planters through training events and through my first book, *Dynamic Church Planting: A Complete Handbook*, which was published in 1992.

In January of 1996 God opened up a training opportunity in St. Petersburg, Russia. For a week we trained Russian nationals in church planting, and equipped other leaders to serve as mentors for church planters. We learned a lot: most of what we taught worked cross-culturally, and some of it did not.

That same year we formed two advisory groups of leaders to help keep us on track with our vision and values. Our on-line international group was called the Worldwide Advisory Group (or WAG). Our face-to-face group of leaders from the United States was called the National Advisory Group (or NAG). We used to joke: Did the WAG wag the NAG? Or did the NAG nag the WAG?

In November of 1996, our National Advisory Group (NAG) counseled us that our 20/20 vision was too small. They pointed out that in only two years our equipping ministry had impacted more than 200 new churches. We were 'way ahead of our current vision statement—to plant 1000 churches by 2020.

The NAG recommended, and our DCPI Board agreed, that DCPI needed to be re-envisioned. The Board gave me the task of praying for God's greater vision for DCPI.

As I begin to pray and think about a new vision, I concluded:

1. Our vision should **consider the need** of the world—for millions of new churches to reach people for Christ.

2. Our vision should **not be limited** by what we think we can do.

3. Vision should rest in what God can do and **must come from Him**.

Once again, I dedicated a personal prayer retreat toward receiving God's new vision for DCPI. That retreat took place on June 13 and 14, 1997.

I spent the first evening and the next morning in a motel room, reading God's word and praying for His vision. On the afternoon of the second day, I drove to Palomar Mountain northeast of San Diego for a hike. I prayed that the Lord would communicate His vision for DCPI, and began the hike.

From the Lower Doan Valley Trail, I veered up the Upper French Valley Trail. The Lord impressed my mind with these words: "Plant a Million Churches." I didn't hear a voice, but the words were imprinted upon my mind.

I kept walking and a few minutes later a second, more complete, phrase came from the Lord: "DCPI will plant a million churches."

I kept hiking and came to an incredibly huge oak tree. This tree is so large that one of the four main branches is thicker than I am tall. The tree is so overarching that the farthest branch shades ground sixty feet from the trunk. But the most unique characteristic of this oak is that its massive trunk rests right on top of a granite boulder. Its roots encircle the boulder and anchor the tree in the ground.

I thought, "This is truly the Oak on the Rock."

While I stared at the tree, amazed, another impression came from the Lord: DCPI will be just like the Oak on the Rock. Just as this tree is founded on a rock, so will DCPI be founded on Jesus Christ, the Rock. "…And on this rock I will build my church" (Mt. 16:18). If DCPI remains founded on Christ, our mission will be like this Oak on the Rock. Now, DCPI is just a three-year old oak sapling. But over time, its growth and influence will be massive and overarching, with many branches of ministry reaching all around the world.

I went home, and in the days following my retreat, kept silent. I didn't talk to anyone because, frankly, I was afraid. I felt uncomfortable with a vision so large that I couldn't see how it could be accomplished. One million churches! How could we ever accomplish this vision?, I wondered. Can we at DCPI carry this vision?

And then one morning during my devotions this thought came to me: "We don't have to carry the vision…God will. And only He can." How true! The Lord gave me His peace, the assurance that I had found His will.

As I wondered how God might fulfill His vision of a million churches, I came to see that this vision is a leadership vision. That's why our strategy statement has remained the same for many years: "Equipping leaders to plant dynamic churches worldwide."

Understanding the Vision of a Million in terms of leadership illustrates how God could fulfill it. You see, there are many Christian leaders throughout the world to whom God has given visions to impact the planting of 100 churches...or a 1000 churches...or more in their lifetimes.

Do the math for each of these scenarios. 1,000,000 churches will be planted when:

a) 100,000 leaders impact 10 churches each.

b) 10,000 leaders impact 100 churches each.

c) 1000 leaders impact 1000 churches each.

The fulfillment of the Vision of a Million will require the realized visions of many other leaders. Early on God showed us a Bible verse that describes the leaders He will call to contribute to this vision: They will be "called oaks of righteousness, a planting of the Lord for the display of his splendor" (Isa. 61:3).

For me, the Vision of a Million was confirmed by an "internal conviction" during my personal prayer time in my office at home on Tuesday morning, June 24, 1997.

I brought the Vision of a Million to the DCPI Board, and some of the members were energized and enthusiastic about the vision. In fact, two of them decided to leave their ministries and join DCPI on full-time staff. But two of my dear friends on the Board thought I was crazy, and brought up some valid concerns.

One Board member said: "We can't be egotistical about this vision. We are not really the ones who are planting these churches. It's the leaders, the mother churches, the associations that we work with who are planting these churches. We have to shine the light on them." So we adjusted our vision statement to begin with this phrase: "Equipping leaders, churches and associations..."

Another Board member added: "How can we possibly aim at the year 2050. That's 53 years from now. The vision will have to be adopted by future generations of leaders if it is to succeed. Can we commit leaders of future generations to our vision?"

We can't, but God can. He will raise up future leaders to bring this vision to pass among future generations. In 1776, when the Declaration of Independence, the

Constitution and the Bill of Rights were established, those leaders committed future generations to the vision of a great nation, the United States of America.

A second leader pointed out, "We aren't planting churches just to be planting churches, but to reach the world for Christ." We all agreed. As a result, we added a final phrase to our vision statement: "…to reach the world for Christ."

Another concern was that a million churches would mean that our mission would have to grow by multiplication, not by addition. That comment helped our mission to become committed to exponential growth.

After six months and three energetic Board meetings, our DCPI Board unanimously adopted the following as our DCPI Vision Statement:

Can we commit leaders of future generations to our vision?

**Equipping leaders, churches and associations
to impact the planting of
One Million Dynamic Churches
to reach the world for Christ!**

What would the world look like if there were another one million dynamic churches?

In his book, *The Purpose Driven Life*, Pastor Rick Warren writes that each human being was created by God to fulfill five purposes:[1]

You were Planned for God's Pleasure (Worship)

You were Formed for God's Family (Fellowship)

You were Created to Become Like Christ (Discipleship)

You were Shaped for Serving God (Ministry)

You were Made for a Mission (Evangelism)

As God fulfills His Vision of a Million Churches through DCPI, hundreds of millions more precious people will experience salvation and live for God's purposes around the globe. They will give God pleasure through worship, and join His family in local congregations. They will become like Christ through discipleship, and serve the Lord in their ministries. And these hundreds of millions of disciples will complete God's mission to win the world for Christ.

As the Great Commission nears its completion, people from every nation, tribe and tongue will have what so many of us already enjoy: a "dynamic" church. In each church, people will experience the caring of an extended family, friends to encourage them, and training to love their spouses and raise their children.

After we adopted our Vision of a Million, our mission really began to accelerate in its productivity and opportunities. We give God all the praise and glory for what He is doing in realizing His vision for our mission.

Since 1995, our DCPI Team has written, published and distributed two church planting Handbooks and ten workbooks on individual topics.

In the summer of 2000 I led five of our DCPI staff to participate in Amsterdam 2000, sponsored by the Billy Graham Evangelistic Association.

11,000 evangelists assembled from all over the world—the largest gathering of its kind in history. DCPI's goal was to develop relationships with 100 international leaders, in the hopes that we might offer them free training and equip them to plant churches.

We knew God was planning something extraordinary when over 100 leaders signed up in just the first hours our booth was open.

For the next nine days, each of our five staff members had a line of leaders waiting to sign up for training. At the end of the conference, 1004 leaders from 72 nations applied to be equipped by DCPI. After the gathering in Amsterdam, leaders continued to network in their own countries and contact us for training until we had 1560 leaders from 82 nations signed up for our church planting training.

What a desperate need there is for training to plant dynamic churches! In the months following the Amsterdam Conference, we continued to meet this need through training events in India, Italy, Myanmar, Nepal, West Africa and the United States.

But we could see that the need far outweighed the capacity of our staff. In 2002, through the influence of DAWN Ministries in Colorado Springs and the Lord's guidance, DCPI began to recruit volunteer Dynamic Associates to bring our training to their countries around the world. A Dynamic Associate is a leader of a church planting movement who has a vision to impact the planting of at least 100 churches in his lifetime and wants to bring DCPI training to his country. We also saw the need to certify trainers in our four tracks of DCPI training for church planters. A Certified Trainer is a gifted trainer and teacher who is equipped by DCPI to train church planting leaders in a specific track of training.

We pray that God will recruit, equip and empower 5000 Dynamic Associates and Certified Trainers in every country of the world. We call this "The Fellowship of the Five Thousand." In four years, the Lord has empowered the DCPI team to recruit and train 181 Dynamic Associates and 476 Certified Trainers from 27 countries and more than 15 of the United States. We praise God for these wonderful leaders and give Him all the glory!

How effectively can the Lord use our Dynamic Associates and Certified Trainers ministries? In 2002, our staff trained 776 church planting leaders. That same year three Dynamic Associates who were also Certified Trainers equipped 1836 leaders. Together, our staff and associates equipped 2612 leaders in India, Nepal, West Africa and the United States. In 2002, we increased the number of leaders trained by 330% over 2001 by including the ministry of our Dynamic Associates.

By the end of 2005, in just the first 11 1/2 years of our new mission, God had equipped more than 15,500 leaders from 67 nations through DCPI. While some of these leaders will never plant a church, others will plant 10 or 100 or even more in their lifetimes. To be conservative, we estimate that for each leader we train, one church will be planted. This means DCPI has impacted the planting of 15,500 churches in our first 11 1/2 years of ministry.

We glorify God for planting these churches!

We are still a long way from fulfilling our Vision of a Million. The ministry must continue to grow exponentially, and there is still much to be done.

It is thrilling to see God fulfilling his vision for our mission. Let's explore some principles that you can use to "See Your Vision Come True!"

[1] Warren, *The Purpose Driven Life*, pp. 320-322.

2

Whose Vision Is It Anyway?

*What is a vision from God? The business world might define a vision as "a mental image produced by the imagination... **seeing** the optimal future for the business and vividly describing this vision."[1] Another business writer suggests "vision is defined as the concept or picture of what your organization can or should be."[2] A vision statement "looks beyond the present to see what could be...what the organization can be at its best."[3]*

Aubrey Malphurs summarizes what this means for those in Christian ministry: a vision is "a clear and challenging picture of the future of a ministry as you believe that it can and must be."[4]

But even if we agree that a vision is a "preferable future," what our church or ministry "can be and must be," we must ask the most important question: Is it your vision, or is it God's vision? It must be a vision from God.

Don't create your own vision. While many Christian leaders do so, it is a recipe for disaster. You will wound yourself and any who follow you. You will end up unfulfilled, frustrated and defeated.

If it's God's vision for your ministry, you have the assurance of being in God's will. And that is the definition of success. You will have the best opportunity to see the vision come true. You also have the guarantee that God will bring his own vision to fulfillment. In Ephesians 2:10 the Bible teaches that "we are God's workmanship, created in Christ Jesus to do good works, which God prepared in advance for us to do." As you seek and discern God's vision for your life and ministry, you can be "confident of this, that he who began a good work in you will carry it on to completion until the day of Christ Jesus. Philippians 1:4-6. In essence, God will complete his own vision for you and your ministry.

So, how can you find out what God's vision for your ministry is? You must find a way to listen to God. And in doing so, you face two major hurdles.

One hurdle to receiving a vision from God can be your belief that you can no longer hear from him. I was teaching on vision in a conservative evangelical seminary some years ago. One of the students raised his hand to say, "We've been taught that God's written Word is the only way he communicates in our day. So, how can you receive a vision from God?"

Have you been taught that you can no longer hear from the Spirit of God, that it is wrong even to try to listen to him? If so, that represents a significant hindrance to receiving God's vision.

God knows his vision for you and your ministry. Stop your frantic "doing."

It's like saying to a soldier in a war: "You have your orders for this battle, the same orders every soldier has received for thousands of years. You won't be hearing from your commanding officer. You are on your own."

And we are in a battle. In fact, it's the greatest war ever fought, a struggle between good and evil. It's the war between the Kingdom of Light and the Kingdom of Darkness. Our commanding officer wants to guide us every step of the way so that we win our battles and avoid the landmines of life.

I love and trust the Bible. I believe it is God's inspired word, an infallible and inerrant revelation of truth. God's word supplies us with eternal principles and examples of God's people who applies those principles. We can always trust the Bible.

But I also believe that the Lord still guides his servants through circumstances, and through his "still, small voice" as we seek him.[5]

Let's take a look at what does the Bible says about trying to listen to God.

In Gen 25:22, Rebekah, Isaac's wife, asked the Lord about the two babies in her womb. The Lord answered: "Two nations are in your womb." The nations were represented by Jacob and Esau.

In Judges 1:1, after the death of Joshua, the Israelites asked the Lord, "Who will be the first to go up and fight for us against the Canaanites? God's specific answer: Judah.

In 2 Samuel 2:1 David brought a question to the Lord. "Shall I go up to one of the towns of Judah?" The Lord answered, Go up. Then David inquired, "Where shall I go?" And the Lord identified Hebron as the specific city.

Why did God direct him to Hebron? Because it was there the Lord would anoint David King over the house of Judah (2 Sam. 2:4). David was living out God's vision for his life.

David was a man after the God's own heart. Perhaps one of the reasons God loved him so much was that David sought his guidance so often.

In these Old Testament examples, God gave specific answers to specific questions. But what about the New Testament? When does God speak in the New Testament?

Jesus anticipated that his followers would want to listen to him. "My sheep listen to my voice; I know them, and they follow me" (Jn. 10:27). Jesus Himself listened to the Father's voice. For example, in John 14: 31, he said "but the world must learn that I love the Father and that I do exactly what my Father has commanded me."

But how did Jesus learn what the Father wanted him to do? He went away to be with his Father alone for extended periods of time. Jesus inquired of God and listened. "Jesus went out into the hills to pray, and spent the night praying to God" (Lk. 6:12).

Or how about the example of the early church in Acts 13:1-3? While the leaders of the new church in Antioch were worshiping the Lord, the Spirit of God communicated to them that Paul and Barnabas were to be their first church planting missionaries.

The second hurdle many of us need to overcome is being willing to hear. We get so preoccupied with what we want to do that we are unwilling to hear God's direction. We are so busy "doing" that we neglect "hearing." We need to carve out from our busy schedules those quiet times to hear the guidance that we so desperately need from God.

In the United States, we have a famous hero whose name is Daniel Boone. He was an outdoorsman, hunter and Congressman. Boone was asked once if he was ever lost while making his way through the wilderness.

"I was never lost," he said. "I was bewildered for about four months one time, but I was never lost."

In other words, he was lost, but just wouldn't admit it!

Men in the United States are often justifiably accused of failing to ask for directions when they are lost while driving. Sometimes, in his confusion, a man will just go faster in the wrong direction.

I have found that when I am lost or confused it is wise to ask for directions as soon as possible from someone who knows the right way. This saves me time and frustration.

Proverbs 1:5 says, "Let the wise listen and add to their learning..."

God knows his vision for you and your ministry. Stop your frantic "doing." Calendar time alone with your Heavenly Father. Listen to God. Hear what he has to say. Ask God for directions all along the journey of your life. Follow His directions for your life, family and ministry. You will be blessed.

Do you want to communicate with God? That is wonderful! But it is also wonderful that God wants to communicate with you even more than you want to communicate with God. Let his Vision be your vision.

[1] http://www.buildingbrands.com/definitions/11_vision_mission.shtml (Accessed February 6, 2006).

[2] http://www.asis.org/Bulletin/Dec-94/ayers.html (Accessed February 6, 2006).

[3] http://www.q4solutions.com/articles/article14-2.html. (Accessed February 6, 2006).

[4] Aubrey Malphurs, Developing a Vision for Ministry in the 21st Century (Grand Rapids: Baker Books, 1999), p. 32.

[5] While I believe you must learn to listen to God, I do not believe the guidance you receive, or think you receive, is "revelation" in a formal sense. The Bible is God's only infallible and inerrant revelation, and I believe the canon is closed. So, as I point out in chapter 3, any guidance you receive must be subject to Scripture and to the wisdom of godly counselors.

3

How to Receive a Vision from God

What is a vision? A vision is a God-given picture of His preferred future for you and your ministry.

How can you receive a vision from God? Spend time alone with God in a prayer retreat or series of prayer retreats. There is no guarantee that God will give you a vision. And certainly he can give you a vision anytime he desires, often when you least expect it. But a prayer retreat is a wonderful spiritual discipline, and a proven way to inquire of God for a vision.

Before I entered the ministry, I was an Outward Bound instructor. Outward Bound is an experiential outdoor education program which utilizes outdoor activities like backpacking, rock climbing, river rafting, and sailing to accomplish goals in the life of the student. These goals would include gaining an appreciation of nature, learning how to work together in a group, and developing an overcoming attitude toward life.

One of the disciplines of the Outward Bound experience is called "the solo." The instructor places each student at an isolated place in the wilderness for three days and two nights, with only a minimum of survival gear. For many people this is the first time they have been completely alone for an extended time.

As an Outward Bound instructor, I enjoyed doing "solos." It was during a solo in the city that I became a Christian.

After I became a Christian, I began to see that my "solos" were actually "duos," because Christ was now involved.

Psalm 139 reminded me, "Where can I go from your Spirit? Where can I flee from your presence? If I go up to the heavens, you are there; if I make my bed in the depths, you are there. If I rise on the wings of the dawn, if I settle on the far side of the sea, even there your hand will guide me, your right hand will hold me fast." God is everywhere!

Incredible! I could spend quality time with the Creator of the Universe who is also my Heavenly Father. He and I could be together, just the two of us, for a time of joyful intimacy and guidance. I could express my deepest thoughts and needs to the One who would understand and meet those needs. I could ask the one who loved me most for the guidance I needed for my life and my family. As a Christian leader, I could inquire of the Master Strategist and receive guidance for my ministry!

I thought, "All Christians and Christian leaders must be doing this." And then I discovered that this was a spiritual discipline practiced by just a few.

How can you receive a vision from God? Learn how to experience an effective prayer retreat. Make this a spiritual discipline. Listen to God and pray for His vision for your life and ministry.

Surely the Lord wants to communicate with you and be with you even more than you want this for yourself.

Isn't it time for you to develop this joyful Christian discipline?

What is a Personal Prayer Retreat[1]

Definition: A personal prayer retreat is a time you set aside to go away to be alone with God.

Let's look at how each phrase clarifies an understanding of a personal prayer retreat.

"A time you set aside"
A personal prayer retreat must be a time that you set aside. It's easy to be trapped into doing the urgent rather than the important. But nothing is more important than spending time with the King of Kings. So if you don't plan for a prayer retreat, you simply won't take one. And you would miss enjoying sweet fellowship with the Lord, and possibly even the vision He has for you and your ministry.

"to go away"
Make sure that you go away for your personal prayer retreat. Trying to "retreat" at home or at the office will be frustrating because of the many distractions.

We live down in the valley — the valley of our everyday lives, where it's too noisy to hear God very well. We need to leave this valley of noise and pressure, and get away to the quiet of God's presence.

That doesn't mean that you have to go far away. The important thing is not distance, but solitude.

"to be alone with God"

This is the essence of a prayer retreat… to be alone with God. In the intimacy of fellowship, your relationship with the Lord will be renewed. You will experience Him. And then you'll ask Him what He wants to do in your personal life, in your family, and in your ministry. So get alone with God and let him reveal what he wants to share with you.

Jeremiah warned against **not** inquiring of God.

"The shepherds are senseless and do not inquire of the Lord, so they do not prosper and all their flock are scattered" (Jer. 10:21). And Isaiah spoke of the blessing of listening to Him: "He wakens me morning by morning, wakens my ear to listen like one being taught. The Sovereign Lord has opened my ears, and **I have not been rebellious; I have not drawn back**" (Isa. 50:5, my emphasis).

We must, absolutely **must**, listen to our God and the Shepherd of our souls!

One obstacle to listening to God may be your own personality.

Introverts draw their energy from being alone, and so prayer retreats are easier to practice. Extroverts are energized from relating to others, and may actually dread being separated from other people. Prayer retreats may be more difficult if you extroverted.

But since our example is Jesus, who withdrew to lonely places to receive guidance from God, prayer retreats are for all of us. Extroverts included.

If you're an extrovert, you may want to include others in your retreats, while still preserving time alone with God. For example, a husband and wife could share a prayer retreat together. A small leadership team could retreat together, but with significant time alone with God for each person.

Twelve Steps to an effective Prayer Retreat

These are tried and true principles
for experiencing an effective prayer retreat.

 Step 1: Go to your retreat site and rest.

The location of your retreat is a matter of personal preference. The real issue is to **go away** to be with the Lord.

Where is the place where you are able to hear from God most effectively? Where can you best become quiet and listen to the Lord? Go there.

Once there, what do you do? If you're like me, you may be exhausted from the pressures of ministry. So first plan to rest.

That was the counsel of Jesus to the apostles:

" The apostles gathered around Jesus and reported to him all they had done and taught. Then, because so many people were coming and going that they did not even have a chance to eat, he said to them, 'Come with me by yourselves to a quiet place and get some rest.' So they went away by themselves in a boat to a solitary place" (Mark 6-30-32).

 Step 2: Pray for your retreat.

James 1:5 is one of our most precious Bible promises. "If any of you lacks wisdom, he should ask God who gives generously to all without finding fault, and it will be given to him."

Wisdom is a great need for all of us, isn't it? We need God's wisdom for the issues, questions and problems we are wrestling with. And we need his wisdom for the direction of our life and ministry. We need his wisdom for his vision. And He has promised to pour out his wisdom for us.

At the beginning of your retreat, you may want to pray like this: "Dear Lord, I pray that you will meet with me and give me your wisdom from the Word and the Holy Spirit as we spend this time together. Help me to plan this retreat so that it accomplishes your purposes in my life and in our time together. I pray in the name and presence and power of Christ. Amen."

Step 3: Plan your retreat.

Because this time is precious, you'll want to be intentional about how you spend it during your retreat. Proverbs 14:22 promises that those who plan what is good find love and faithfulness.

So lay out, step by step, what you are going to be doing during your retreat time. These twelve steps are one plan, but certainly not the only one. Let the Lord lead you—adapt your plan based on your needs.

For example, how is God leading you? And how much time do you have? The same plan that you use for a three-day retreat will not work if you have only six hours.

If your purpose it to seek the Lord for his vision for your life and ministry, that will be uppermost in your planning and your prayers.

 Step 4: Repent of your sins.

Sin will obstruct your receiving God's guidance or enjoying His fellowship, so first repent and receive His cleansing.

Jesus said, "Those whom I love I rebuke and discipline. So be earnest, and repent. Here I am! I stand at the door and knock. If anyone hears my voice and opens the door, I will come in and eat with him, and he with me" (Rev. 3:19, 20).

Verse 20 is often used as salvation verse, but it speaks more directly to Christ's desire for fellowship with the believer. He is knocking on the door of your heart. Repenting of your sins assures He will enter the door of intimate fellowship with you, ready to communicate and guide.

 Step 5. Thankfully review how God has been working.

For years my early morning devotions have included a daily recording of praises for who God is and thanksgiving for what he does. Then on my prayer retreats, I look back over the months to see how God is working.

I spend time worshiping the Lord, enjoying His presence and praising His character. As much as you long to discover vision for your life and ministry, your overarching purpose is to be alone with Him—to love and praise him and experience his glory.

Praising and thanking him prepares you, as Henry Blackaby's Experiencing God has pointed out, to join God in what he is doing, rather than asking him to join you!

Step 6: Submit to God's plans for you.

As we prepare for our retreats, we may already be thinking of our own plans and preferences. Sometimes our plans emerge from impure motives. The sad result may be that we end up with our plans instead of God's plans for us.

Proverbs 19:21 counsels us, "Many are the plans in a man's heart, but it is the LORD'S purpose that prevails."

Receiving God's vision must begin by submitting to His plans, whatever those may be. Sincerely pray a prayer like this one:

"Lord, I willingly submit to your plans for my life. I know that you have my best interests at heart. You can see the end from the beginning. I want what you want for my life. I trust you. In Jesus' name, Amen."

 Step 7: Devour the word of God and take notes.

Often God guides us directly from his word. "Your word is a lamp to my feet and a light for my path," promises Ps. 119:105. Specific books of the Bible may meet specific needs as you practice the discipline of prayer retreats.

For example, Proverbs and Nehemiah have often been incredibly helpful when I am planning, team building, or facing opposition in ministry.

Ask God to guide you into the right books of the Bible to read for your retreat. Then take notes as you read and read and read some more. Often God will bring verses back to you during your listening time.

 Step 8: Write down your specific issues and questions.

What are the specific issues and questions that you really need to hear from God about?

For my prayer retreats, I have three categories of issues and questions: personal, family, and ministry. And if your retreat is focused on receiving God's vision for your ministry, that will lead you to other specific questions.

Here are some sample questions and issues that you may consider for a prayer retreat:

Personal:
What do you want me to do now to strengthen my spiritual life
and keep it vital?
What happens next with my exercise and eating plan?

Family:

What do you want me to do to help my spouse and enhance our marriage?

What do you want me to do to prepare my children well for their lives?

Ministry:

What is the next step in our ministry and how do you want to bring it to pass?

Who do you have in mind to help us with our ministry?

Vision for the future:

What are the gifts, abilities and passions you have given me to use for your glory?

How shall I use these to honor you in the future? What's next for me as I serve you?

Step 9: Meet with God in a quiet place. Listen and take notes.

Consider Elijah, who was discouraged, and needed guidance from God. He found his quiet place in a cave (1 Kings 19:9-13). He discovered the Lord spoke, not in a great wind, earthquake, or fire, but in a gentle whisper.

I find I can best hear God's "still, small voice" as I hike by myself in the mountains. While my body is engaged in exercise, my mind and spirit connect with the Lord. I take along a small notebook or cards to take notes as he gives me insights and "consecrated thoughts."

For example, here are some of the thoughts I recorded on a prayer walk:

> My kids need to know how much I love and appreciate them…especially now. They need to know they can come to me to get their needs met.

> Reconcile with a couple.

> You must love your staff.

I call them "consecrated" thoughts because my thinking process has been set apart, dedicated, sanctified to the Lord by all the steps leading up to my listening prayer time.

Step 10: Prayerfully respond in writing to your questions and issues.

After I return to my retreat site, I transfer my notes to my laptop computer. Then I try to match my thoughts with the issues and questions I recorded earlier. Often I discover questions for which I haven't yet received specific guidance. So I continue to think, and then record these thoughts, too. Because God has prepared me, I am able to do my clearest planning during this time.

 Step 11: Receive counsel from wise, godly people.

Trying to listen to God has its pitfalls. You could be wrong. Even after repentance and submission, your motives could be impure. You could be hearing what you want to hear. You could have had a bad dinner the night before.

The Lord gives us his sobering perspective on lying prophets:

> " I have heard what the prophets say who prophesy lies in my name. They say, 'I had a dream! I had a dream!' How long will this continue in the hearts of these lying prophets, who prophesy the delusions of their own minds?... I am against the prophets who wag their own tongues and yet declare, 'The LORD declares.' Indeed, I am against those who prophesy false dreams... They tell them and lead my people astray with their reckless lies, yet I did not send or appoint them. They do not benefit these people in the least," declares the LORD (Jer. 23:25, 31, 32).

Counsel from wise godly people is a solution to this pitfall. "Plans fail for lack of counsel, but with many advisers they succeed." (Proverbs 15:22).

Run your guidance from God through the grid of wisdom from godly leaders.

 Step 12: Plan to communicate your thoughts and delegate tasks.

As you consider your thoughts and decisions, ask yourself, Who needs to know?

To whom do I need to communicate these thoughts? Family members? Church leaders? Friends?

If God has given me the beginning of a new vision, who among your trusted counselors and friends should you share with first?

Jethro, Moses' father-in-law, taught a great lesson in delegation in Exodus 18. His point? We wear ourselves out if we try to do everything ourselves. We need to get organized and entrust ministry to reliable people.

So plan your communication and delegation. Who needs to do what? How will you communicate this to them?

Challenge

On May 26, 1998, Tom Whittaker, a college instructor from Arizona, succeeded in climbing Mount Everest. Completing this climb would have been an incredible achievement for anyone, but even more so for Tom. And not just because it was his third attempt, or that he was 50 years old, or that he overcame altitude sickness. What was most remarkable is that Tom Whittaker climbed Everest using an artificial limb.

On June 30, 2004, I fulfilled a life goal by standing on top of Mount Kilimanjaro in Tanzania which at 19,300 feet in elevation is the highest mountain in Africa. It was the most difficult physical challenge in my life. I know from climbing Mount Kilimanjaro and other peaks that mountain climbing involves hard work, suffering and joy. Tom's hard work and suffering must have been incredible. But he believed it was worth it.

How much effort are you willing to invest to receive a vision from God?

As I look back on 29 years of ministry, every life-changing decision that was made for our family and our ministry emerged from a prayer retreat. Dynamic Church Planting International (DCPI) was born in a prayer retreat. And, as I have shared, DCPI's "Vision of a Million" came from a prayer retreat.

The Lord Jesus taught us to pray, "Thy Kingdom come, Thy will be done on earth as it is in heaven." As a Christian leader, how can you best use the gifts and experience and passion he has given you to advance his kingdom?

My challenge to you is to set aside at least two personal prayer retreats every year. Times to get away and get with God. Times to listen, plan, and obey.

If you do, the Lord will give you the guidance and vision you seek. As He gives you direction, you will have more internal conviction about implementing His vision and more confidence that you are doing the right thing. You will have a greater potential to succeed in your personal, family and ministry life. You will see your vision come true!

 *Will you commit to taking at least two prayer retreats each year?*

[1] DCPI publishes an expanded version of this chapter, called "How to Take an Effective Personal Prayer Retreat." Available at www.dcpi.org.

4

How to Refine Your Vision

*Now, it is time to refine your vision. The word "refine" has
a variety of meanings and synonyms. To refine means to
purify, to filter out contaminates and to get rid of
impurities. When crude oil is processed at a "refinery" it
becomes gasoline that we can use to power our car. When
gold ore goes through the process of "refining" the
impurities are removed and it becomes pure gold.*

Your vision needs to be refined. Improved. Purified. Made usable. Here are some steps in the process of refining your vision.

1. Confirm Your Vision through Prayer

In 1997, when I received the vision that DCPI was to impact the planting of a million churches, I did not rush right home and tell everybody. What if I hadn't heard the Lord accurately? What if I had heard only what I wanted to hear? I needed affirmation from the Lord if this was indeed his vision for our mission.

So, I prayed about the vision during my morning devotional times: "Lord, is this really your vision for our mission?" I prayed that morning after morning. And then I would listen.

I prayed about it for at least a month. One morning, I had a strong inner conviction and a peace, a confirmation, that this indeed was God's vision for our mission. I remember crying out to God, "I can't carry this vision. It is too big for me." The Lord's assurance came to me: "You don't have to carry it. I'll carry it. It is my vision for the mission."

After you have received the basic vision from the Lord, you should pray about it on a daily basis asking the Lord to affirm the vision. As you come to Him each day, humble and open in prayer, I am confident the Lord will give you the confirmation you need.[1]

2. Shape the Vision through the Counsel of Key Leaders

The next step is to communicate your vision to your Key Leaders. After the Lord had confirmed the vision, I called a DCPI Board Meeting and shared it with them. The Board of Directors of DCPI is directly accountable to God for our mission. If we were going to adopt a new vision for our mission, they were the Key Leaders who needed to shape and adopt it.

As I shared the Vision of a Million, I wondered if some of our Board Members would think I was crazy. Two of them did! But what I didn't anticipate was what a powerful motivator a God- given vision would be for other leaders.

Two other Board members got so excited that they became full-time staff members. One of those staff members is Dr. Mark Williams. During the last 8 years, as our Vice President of Training, Mark has impacted the planting of many thousands of new churches in Africa, Canada, Europe, India, Myanmar, Nepal, Pakistan and the United States of America. Now that is Kingdom Impact!

But back to the Board members who thought I was crazy. One of them said, "We at DCPI are not the ones who are really planting the churches. The leaders, churches and associations are planting the churches." And so we added a phrase at the beginning of our vision statement: "*to equip leaders, churches, and associations* to impact the planting of a million dynamic churches."

Another Board member said, "We are not just planting churches as an end in itself. Our ultimate goal is to reach the world for Christ." And so we placed that phrase at the end of our mission statement: "to equip leaders, churches and associations to impact the planting of one million dynamic churches *to reach the world for Christ.*"

These leaders, especially the ones who originally thought I was crazy, really helped to shape the final vision statement. Through the wisdom that God gave to them, they made the final result better.

I recommend sharing with your leaders one-on-one before you present your vision to the gathered board or leadership team. Don't surprise them in a group with a new and challenging idea before they've had time individually to think about it, share concerns, and provide input.

For example, take your Board Chairman out to lunch and share the vision. Meet with a key influencer on the Board at his home and get his input on the vision first. Once you get "buy in" from the key leaders individually, your presentation to the full group will more likely result in faith, unity, and courage.

So begin thinking of the individuals who can help you share your vision statement. Who can help? A mentor? Your Board members? Wise counselors? Friends in other churches or ministries? Gifted writers and editors? Ask them to help you to produce the best result.

3. Boil it down into a Concise, Motivational Vision Statement

When you boil down a liquid, the water becomes steam and you are left with just the very essence in the pot. Boil the vision down into a concise, motivational statement. You want it to communicate God's preferred future for your ministry clearly, simply and powerfully.

During three Board meetings over four months, our Directors prayed about and discussed our new vision statement. The Lord brought us to the place of unity in which we were unanimous in affirming our new vision statement:

"Equipping leaders, churches and associations

to impact the planting

of one million dynamic churches

to reach the world for Christ"

Here are some other examples of vision statements:

- My pastor, Hal Seed, jumped out of bed one morning with the words of New Song Church's vision statement on his heart: **"A Great Front Door and a Great Serving Core."**

- This next vision statement is from Our Place Christian Church in Portland, Oregon: **Enjoy Life. Experience God. Equip Each Other. Expand God's Kingdom.**

- NorthStar Community Church, Maryland, USA, focuses on this as their purpose: NorthStar Community Church will be **a place where you will feel comfortable, loved and accepted for who you are, as you change and grow into what God wants you to be.**

- Ken Blanchard Companies, founded by Christian corporate trainer, Ken Blanchard gives this as their mission: *to help the organizations we work with unleash the power and potential of the people in their organizations for the common good.*

- DAWN Ministries is a worldwide Christian parachurch movement. Their mission is to *see saturation church planting become the generally accepted and fervently practiced strategy for completing the task of making disciples of all people in our generation.*

- Wycliffe's mission is to *assist the church in making disciples of all nations through Bible translation.*

- Christian Outreach Centre in Australia does three things: *Win the lost and make disciples. Empower leaders. Multiply healthy churches.*

- Mission One Million is a Christian ministry devoted to *reaching one million orphans, supporting one million indigenous missionaries, and building one million churches in the least evangelized, most populated and poorest third-world countries.*

- Project Brazil 2010 wants to see *A Church within Access of Everyone in Brazil in this Generation.*

- Outreach, Inc., a Christian business, wants to *create a network of churches and ministries working together to invite and connect every person in America to a bible believing church and ultimately into a personal relationship with Jesus Christ.*

What is your concise, motivational vision statement? Ask God's help to do this. Using 20 words or less, write down your motivational vision statement.

In order to refine your vision, you have:

> Confirmed Your Vision through Prayer

> Shaped the Vision through the Counsel of Key Leaders

> Boiled it down into a Concise, Motivational Vision Statement

Now, you are ready to communicate your vision.

[1] Of course it is possible the Lord will not provide the confirmation of inner peace about your vision. If that should happen, return to a season of waiting upon Him. Reread chapter 3, and begin again to seek the vision He has for you and your ministry.

5

Communicate the Vision to the Right People

As you communicate your vision story and statement, people will respond in three ways. They will…

1. **think** the vision is foolish and dislike it.

2. be apathetic and ignore it.

3. **catch** the vision and love it.

Just be patient. Some people may take some time to become convinced. You need to find the people who, over time, will catch your vision, love your vision and get excited about it. These are the ones who will want to work with you to see your vision fulfilled.

God will bring the right people to stand with you to see your vision become reality.

Remember, Jesus said, "No one can come to me unless the Father who sent me draws him…(John 6:44). And later he promised, "But I, when I am lifted up from the earth, I will draw all men to myself" (John 12:32). The Lord is always drawing people to himself. And I believe that God also draws people to the visions that he gives to his leaders on earth.

While there is no strict order you must follow, ask the Lord for which leaders to approach first. Here are some suggestions.

Get your Board "on board."

As I pointed out in the last chapter, start with your Key Influencers on the Board. Then, let them help you gain the support of the rest of the Board. Your Board should next help you to craft your vision story and statement.

Remember, your Board will need time to pray, to process the vision, to ask questions and receive answers. Of course you, as the visionary leader, are already completely committed and ready to move forward. Your impulse will be to run ahead of your leaders.

But don't lose patience. Gently and lovingly help them through the process. When your Board is committed, you will have top-level leaders who are standing with you to communicate, provide for and defend the vision.

Ask your Prayer Team to intercede for the vision.

God loves to fulfill his own visions in his own time, and God loves to answer prayer. So ask your prayer warriors to pray both that God will fulfill his vision, and also that he will reveal the next step for that vision.

Dr. Mark Williams began his DCPI ministry as our Director of Daughter Church Planting. He had planted two churches, which had impacted the planting of four daughter churches. When he and I were ready to start writing The Dynamic Daughter Church Planting Handbook, he had his prayer team praying for that book. It was published in 1999 and was the next step toward our Vision of a Million.

How thrilled your prayer team will be when they see the Lord answer their prayers and complete the next step toward your vision!

Recruit and keep Staff focused with your vision.

The vision is one of your most powerful tools for recruiting staff members. One leader said to me while I was recruiting him, "Your vision and values are my vision and values." He joined our staff.

A second powerful tool for recruiting other leaders is the Position Description. This document, which outlines the particular responsibilities of each staff role, reveals how every position helps fulfill your ministry's vision. For example, at DCPI the role of Vice President of Training is essential to a vision dedicated to equipping leaders.

You need to help the leaders you are recruiting make the connection between the role they would be accepting and the accomplishment of the overall vision.

Just recently, as I was recruiting a leader, I shared with him the eight positions we had available. But foolishly, I talked mainly about the one for which he seemed most suited.

His wife laughed and said that he couldn't possibly do that job. He agreed and laughed as well. Then, he said, "Tell me more about the Vice President of

Development." I talked to him about serving our donors and raising finances for our mission. He said, "I can do that!"

Your vision will also help you to keep your staff focused. It keeps the main thing the main thing. It keeps you from doing good ministry that is not your best ministry. Your ministry becomes more of a rifle shot than a shotgun blast.

A vision motivates Donors to invest.

People prefer to make financial investments in organizations that have a vision. They want to know where your church or ministry is headed before they commit financially. They want a picture of the preferred future.

Recently, I was having breakfast with the CEO of a multi-million dollar corporation who is also a major donor of DCPI's. I asked him, "What is it about DCPI that God has used to motivate you to invest financially in our mission?" He said, "It is your God-sized vision and the way that God is bringing it about."

In DCPI's basic church planting training, the participants' final assignment is to present their V-P-T, or Vision-Plan-Timeline, for their new church. We know that once church planters can articulate their vision, they will find it much easier to attract donors and other potential partners, like denominational and mother church leaders.

Reach your Target Group with your vision.

What is your target group? Who is God calling you to help? You may be planting a church to reach un-churched people. Or maybe you're the pastor of an established church and you really want to help them become solid disciples of Christ. Perhaps you're leading a rescue mission in an inner city? You could even be involved in a mission to train leaders like we are at DCPI.

Our target group is part of our purpose statement: *Equipping **leaders** to plant dynamic churches worldwide.*

We know we're "targeting" Christian leaders involved in church planting. As we communicate our purpose and vision statements, they know we are in business to equip them.

In chapter one, I shared with you what God did when our team attended Amsterdam 2000. We believed that some of the 11,000 evangelists who gathered there would be church planters. Before we went, we set a goal to offer free church planting training to 100 third-world evangelists.

When the attendees learned that we were a mission dedicated to equipping church planters, we were overwhelmed with 1004 applications for training. These leaders represented 72 nations.

When your vision coincides with a strong felt need on the part of your target group, amazing things can happen!

Encourage volunteers to help bring the vision to pass.
Volunteerism is on the rise. Many people want to volunteer their time and energy to a significant cause.

Christian leader, if God has given you a vision, there are almost certainly people in your relationships and community who want to volunteer to help you realize that vision. Find those people and communicate your vision. Let them help you in a way that works for you and for them.

Find Partners who have the same heart for your vision.
Who can partner with you to see your vision come true?

"It is your God-sized vision and the way that God is bringing it about."

Who can help you? Who can mentor you? Encourage you? Show you new ways to get things done? Who are your peers who have the same heart as you do for your vision? They may be serving in their own churches or organizations. These people may be in the same city. Or they may be serving half way around the world from where you are.

God blesses unity among his people. "May the God who gives endurance and encouragement give you a spirit of unity among yourselves as you follow Christ Jesus, so that with one heart and mouth you may glorify the God and Father of our Lord Jesus Christ" (Romans 15:5-6).

In our mission at Dynamic Church Planting International, we believed that there were thousands of leaders around the world to whom God had given a unified call to equip church planters and establish one million churches.

We knew that our vision could not be accomplished by our Board and staff...that we would need thousands of partners around the world who shared our vision.

This gave birth to a team we call The Fellowship of the Five Thousand. God is calling out from among his people an army of five thousand leaders who deeply desire to reach every nation of the world for Christ through church planting training. We learned that a national leader can reach his nation much better than someone from outside his culture. This gave birth to the ministries of Dynamic Associates and Certified Trainers.

A Dynamic Associate is a visionary church planting leader who wants to bring DCPI training to his country or culture. A Certified Trainer is a gifted teacher who is equipped and certified to teach one or more of DCPI's tracks of training.

By 2020, there will be 5000 Dynamic Associates and Certified Trainers equipping church planting leaders in every country of the world. It will truly be The Fellowship of the Five Thousand. These leaders and trainers will be within easy access of every church planter around the globe. Church planters will no longer be lonely or isolated. Dynamic Associates and Certified Trainers will work together to actively train church planters. They will lead growing church planting missions. They will write books and produce resources that help church planting leaders. As a result, in 2020, every church planter in the world will have the opportunity to be trained and mentored to establish a dynamic church.

DCPI just started the Dynamic Associates and Certified Trainer ministry in 2003. By God's grace, at this writing in October 2006, there are already 476 Certified Trainers and 181 Dynamic Associates who live in 27 countries and 15 US states. The Lord may be touching your heart to become a member of The Fellowship of the Five Thousand. He may be motivating you to help establish one million new churches. You may want to bring DCPI training to your country or culture. If so, contact DCPI through our website at **www.dcpi.org** or email us at **service@dcpi.org**.

Who needs to become a part of your vision? Who are your "right people?" Make a list of the groups. Make a list of individual people in the groups with whom you need to communicate your vision. Communicate your vision. Go do it!

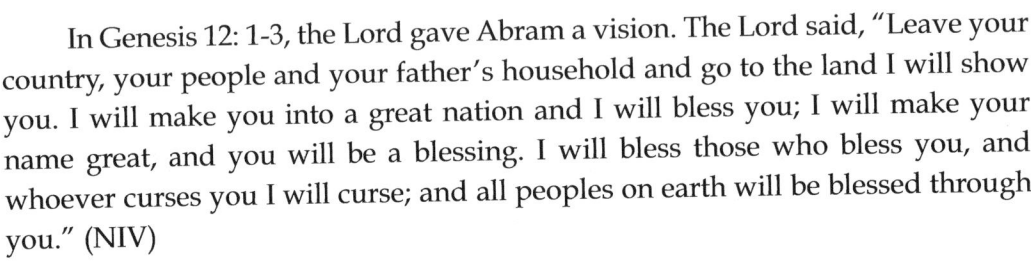

6

How to Communicate Your Vision

One of your responsibilities as the bearer of a vision from God is to communicate that vision.

In Genesis 12: 1-3, the Lord gave Abram a vision. The Lord said, "Leave your country, your people and your father's household and go to the land I will show you. I will make you into a great nation and I will bless you; I will make your name great, and you will be a blessing. I will bless those who bless you, and whoever curses you I will curse; and all peoples on earth will be blessed through you." (NIV)

Abram's vision was to be a blessing not only to him but to all the families of the earth. The vision that the Lord gives to you will be a blessing to others as well.

It is vital that you communicate your vision to others so that God will bless others with your vision.

Communicating your vision is an ongoing responsibility, not just a one-time event. As long as you are the directional leader, you will need to lift up the vision.

People lose sight of the big picture quickly. Some leaders say that people can lose the vision in as little as two weeks. So keep telling your story!

Charting your progress toward fulfilling the vision is another way of communicating that vision. Your supporters need to know and deserve to know about this progress. Is the vision really coming to pass? As you complete a year of ministry, be sure to update everyone involved in the vision.

Use monthly communiqués (including email and paper mail) to demonstrate your progress. These will encourage your people and give your ministry credibility. Donors will be inspired to give and staff members will work harder and with more joy. Telling your story and the progress you're making toward the vision will help you in many other ways, including recruitment.

So what are some ways that you can communicate your vision?

Tell and write the story of your vision.

In Jerusalem, Paul told the story of his encounter with Jesus: "About noon as I came near Damascus, suddenly a bright light from heaven flashed around me. I fell to the ground and heard a voice say to me, 'Saul! Saul! Why do you persecute me?' 'Who are you, Lord?' I asked. 'I am Jesus of Nazareth, whom you are persecuting,' he replied. My companions saw the light, but they did not understand the voice of him who was speaking to me.

'What shall I do, Lord?' I asked. 'Get up,' the Lord said, ' and go into Damascus. There you will be told all that you have been assigned to do'" (Acts 22:6-10). Again, in Acts 26, before King Agrippa, Paul told the story of his vision.

Write down your vision story. Make sure the details are accurate and practice telling it. Then share the story of your vision from God over and over again. Most people love to listen to compelling stories.

Always be ready to share your vision story. Tell it to individuals and tell it to small groups. And when God gives you opportunity before a large gathering, tell your story.

Your story will reach into the hearts of the people whom God has chosen to help you.

As you write out your vision story, include pictures and photos and graphics when possible. Use your vision story in brochures and newsletters and in email messages. Be sure to highlight your vision statement throughout your ministry.

Put your vision on your website and send it out via email.

One of the great opportunities we have today is to communicate via the internet. You can share your vision with an email group. I have been doing this in a message called "From My Heart to Yours." Keep your emails short and sweet. Aim for one page in length.

Put your vision statement and your vision story on your website. Make it easy for people to respond to you. The Lord may want them to help you realize the vision.

Use symbols to communicate your vision.

Symbols have often helped communicate our faith. Moses lifted up a serpent in the wilderness as a symbol of God's power to forgive and heal (Number 21:1-9). Jesus Himself used this image to summarize his own saving mission (John 3:14-15).

The sign of the cross has symbolized Christianity for centuries. The "fish" emblem of the early Christians was a clever acrostic that used the Greek letters for fish ("ixthus") as shorthand for "Jesus Christ, God's Son, Savior."

So what kind of objects can communicate your vision?

At DCPI we use a tree, called the Oak on the Rock. As I described in chapter one, the Lord actually used this tree to communicate his vision for DCPI to me. As I was hiking in the mountains on a prayer retreat in the mountains, the Lord gave me these words: "DCPI will plant a million churches."

Soon after I came to the huge oak tree we now call "The Oak on the Rock." And there the Lord showed me how this immense tree, with its far-reaching branches, is like the vision he has for DCPI to have an impact around the world.

An object, a symbol, a tree, is not the vision, of course. But it represents and communicates the vision. When you see our DCPI logo, you are looking at an actual line drawing of the Oak on the Rock. What is the symbol of your vision?

Have your staff and key leaders memorize your vision statement.

Memorizing scripture is a powerful way to permeate our hearts with God's Word. "I seek you with all my heart; do not let me stray from your commands. I have **hidden your word in my heart** that I might not sin against you" (Ps 119:10-11).

The same is true for the vision that God has given you. It will help you and your leaders stay on the same track if you memorize your vision.

Be sure to lead by example: you must memorize your vision statement. Don't expect any one else to memorize it unless you do. Then require that your staff memorize your vision. Ask your Board and Key Leaders to do the same.

Repeat your vision frequently and passionately.

If it's true that people lose vision in about two weeks, it makes sense to bring special attention to your vision at least once every two weeks.

There is no substitute for passion. Are you passionate about your vision? Are you in awe over your encounter with God? Does that come out in the excitement and conviction in your speaking and writing? Yes, some people will think you are crazy. That is OK. Be passionate about your vision! Get animated!

Be creative in communicating your vision.
Of course with frequent repetition comes the risk of boring people, so that they fail to really listen.

So how can we communicate both consistently *and creatively* so we don't bore our listeners?

Sow the vision in interesting ways. Sometimes go through the "back door," rather than the "front door." In other words, take an indirect approach rather than a direct one at times when you are communicating the vision.

During the fall of 2002, I received an email from a Kenyan church planter whom we had trained 16 months before in Italy.

Dear Rev. Paul,

Choice Christian greetings in Jesus name. My name is Rev. Jonathan Eric Mudenyo from Webuye, Kenya (Africa). I attended the DCPI conference in Rimini, Italy last year and was so much blessed. I came back home and began conducting the conference on small scale to most of my fellow ministers in church. Since I came back last June, I have planted 12 churches and they are all doing so well. The materials that I brought home with me have been very helpful and I have used them to train others.

It really works.

Please, I kindly write to invite DCPI to conduct yet another conference in Nairobi, Kenya, to help in equipping the body of Christ in Africa.

God bless you.

Pastor Jonathan Eric Mudenyo

I simply forwarded this email to the people who need to hear the DCPI vision again in a fresh way. What a great reminder that God is using our mission to make progress toward his vision.

Our focus should always be on what God is doing to accomplish his vision. Yes, you are the steward of the vision, but it comes from God and he is the only one who can bring it to pass. Since it is his vision, he must get all the glory!

So what are some ways you can creatively communicate the vision?

1. Testimonies of people who have been impacted by your vision communicate in a powerful way. Let them tell their story "live and in person," or through written testimony in email or newsletters. Like the email from Pastor Mudenyo, this is a great way to share God at work fulfilling his vision.

2. Our church uses dramas during worship services to effectively communicate our pastor's vision of a "Great front door and a great serving core".

3. The right song or video can touch a person's heart deeply. Have you noticed that when a filmmaker wants to touch you with the primary point of a movie, he will use music to grab your emotions? I can think of several movies that had me weeping at the end. It was a combination of the movie's message and the music that brought me to tears. You may want to create a short 8 minute video about your ministry that you can place on CD's and send to key leaders and supporters.

4. Your office space can cast vision for you. When you walk into DCPI Headquarters in Oceanside, California, your eyes are drawn to the wall in front of you. Raised black letters proclaim, "*Our Vision*: Equipping leaders, churches and associations to plant one million dynamic churches to reach the world for Christ."

You look to your left and see *a huge map* of the world.

Then, as you enter the main room, you are once again captured by more raised letters—"*Our Strategy*: Equipping leaders to plant dynamic churches worldwide." Below that is a cabinet full of DCPI books and workbooks used to do that equipping.

Right there is also our **DCPI MasterPlanning Arrow** that communicates how we believe God is going to fulfill the Million Church vision.

Next, you could enter the Global Room. You would see an entire wall covered by a 10' map of the world.

When you visit our office, you see God's vision for our mission and how He is fulfilling this vision one step at a time. God has done all this, and we give him all the glory

5. Banners can also tell the vision story. Some years ago, I attended the birth service of a new church in a high school in Washington State. They proclaimed their vision statement with a gigantic banner across the top of the wall in the front of the school stage. There was no doubt about where they believed God was taking them.

Communicate your vision! Tell and write the vision story. Communicate your vision through symbols. Have your key leaders memorize the vision statement. Passionately repeat your vision in creative ways over and over and over again.

7

Use Your Vision to Plan Your Work

Failing to plan is a major pitfall for many visionary leaders. They may rationalize like this: "God has given me a vision. I don't need to plan anything, because the Holy Spirit will bring the vision to pass. In fact, planning isn't very spiritual anyway."

But the truth is, if you fail to plan, you plan to fail. Many visions have been lost at this stage.

God wants you to win through planning!

Just what does the Bible say about planning? Consider these examples:

1. Jesus Himself taught planning when He said, "Suppose one of you wants to build a tower. Will he not first sit down and estimate the cost to see if he has enough money to complete it?" (Luke 14:28) .

2. "We should make plans . . . counting on God to direct us" (TLB), counsels Proverbs 16:9. No plan should be made without God's direction. But God directs planning, not just spontaneous efforts.

3. Proverbs 11:14 says, "For want of a skillful strategy an army is lost; victory is the fruit of long planning" (NEB). Visions have literally been lost "for want of a skillful strategy." A leader's heart may be right, his efforts diligent and goals noble. But without careful planning, the battle can be lost.

The Lord wants us to *plan*!

Dr. Mark Williams is Vice President of Training with DCPI. Previously, he served as the founding pastor of two churches. Listen to Mark's story, in his own words.

" The first church we started was started with no Vision, TaskList or TimeLine. We started with thirteen people in attendance on the first Sunday, and very slowly grew from there. We planned as we went along, and the fruit was limited.

The second church was started with a carefully planned Vision, TaskList and TimeLine. The foundation was laid out over a period of several months. On launch Sunday there were 225 people in attendance, most of whom came because of our outreach planning and efforts. Thirteen people were saved on the first Sunday! Over the next three years, 127 people professed faith in Christ."

Having done it "both ways," Mark believes that it is a lot more productive, enjoyable and God-honoring to carefully plan out the work of church planting.

If God is not at work, even the best-laid plans will fail. But if God is in the vision, we can serve Him best by *prayerful planning*.

The bottom line: God's vision must lead to prayerful planning, the result of which should be a comprehensive TaskList set out upon a TimeLine.

Write down your Strategic Plan

Do not just point to your head and say "It is all up here and that is good enough." It is not good enough. It is vitally important that you write down your Strategic Plan.

In 1997, the Lord gave us our DCPI Vision. During the remainder of that year, I worked with our Board of Directors to fine-tune the DCPI Vision statement and come to a unanimous agreement. Just as a reminder, our DCPI Vision Statement is: "Equipping leaders, churches, and associations to impact the planting of one million dynamic churches to reach the world for Christ."

My next major question was: "Now, what is our plan?" I carved out four days for a personal Prayer and Planning Retreat at a hotel in Chicago, Illinois, USA. I took three books:

1. **The Bible** to keep me on track with God's will.

2. **Built to Last** by James C. Collins and Jerry I. Porras. I wanted to incorporate the successful habits of visionary companies in our organization. You can find this very valuable book at www.harpercollins.com.

3. **Master-planning** by Bobb Biehl. It is subtitled "The Complete Guide for Building a Strategic Plan for Your Business, Church or Organization." That statement is true in my experience.

I studied *Master-planning* during that retreat, and then followed Bobb's instructions. At the end of the retreat, I had a Strategic Plan that I could communicate to my Board and Staff teams. I regard Bobb Biehl as the "master planner" in the Christian community. I highly recommend that you buy his book. Read, study and use it. You will be blessed and so will your Staff, Board and those whom you are serving. To order it and other resources, go to their website at: www.masterplanninggroup.com/

Another great resource for planning is the Microsoft Project software program. It will help you to identify tasks and assign them to people. You can work with the software to automatically place your tasks on a timeline. To purchase the program, go to www.microsoft.com.

Here is a simple outline for your Strategic Plan. Within each division of the plan are included some questions and action steps. Your answers to these questions and your written responses to these action steps will form the basis of your Strategic Plan. In the Appendix of this book, you will find this Strategic Planning Tool in a form that you can use.

VISION:

Prepare a written statement of your unique vision. (Describe in concrete terms what this idealized picture looks like).

Who are you trying to help?

What are their needs?

How will you meet their needs?

What values will your organization embrace?

What are your organization's name, logo, and slogan?

Describe the number and type of staff that your organization will require.

 PLAN:

Describe your personal role in the vision.

What are your goals? Short term (90 days). Medium term (90 days to 2 years). Long Term (2 years to 50 years).

Describe the steps that you need to take in order to share the vision and gain ownership by the appropriate decision makers.

What objections to your vision do you anticipate? How will you answer them?

What roadblocks to implementing your vision and plan will you encounter? How will you overcome these roadblocks?

What resources will your organization need and where will you find them?

How will you recruit, assess and equip the staff?

How much will your vision cost? Formulate a first draft of a proposed budget (including startup expenses for the first year before birth).

What means will you pursue to financially support yourself, the staff and the project?

 **TIMELINE**

Make a comprehensive list of the action steps you and your team need to take in order to accomplish each short term and medium term goal?

Place your tasks on your TimeLine.

Use your vision to plan your work. Planning is affirmed in scripture as a very valuable practice. Write down your Strategic Plan. Use proven books, resources and leaders to help you prepare well for the future. Plan to win! And keep planning to win year after year by continuing to plan!

8

Use Your Vision to Work Your Plan

Many leaders develop a fine vision statement and construct an elegant plan. But then they stumble into another pitfall: They fail to work their plan.

Your vision is like a compass for a traveler who is walking through a wilderness where there are no trails. If the traveler is lost and doesn't know the right way, he takes his compass out of his pocket and holds it in front of him. *The magnetic needle inside the compass points due north.*

You turn your body to orient the compass needle to due north. If you want to travel due north, you look up and find an object off in the distance like a mountain or a tree or a lake that is due north and you walk in that direction. A compass is worthless unless you actually use it to walk to your goal. A vision is worthless unless you work your plan and move toward your goal.

Work Your Plan

Take the action steps that you have on your TimeLine to accomplish your goals. As the NIKE slogan goes: ***"Just Do It!"***

Recruit the staff! Gather the core team! Raise the money! Find the facility! Create or adapt that program! Get your Board on board. Pray your way through that obstacle. Cast the vision! Write that email! Make that phone call! Do what you know you have to do. Do not be thwarted. Remember: God has given you a vision. See your vision come true!

As you take these important action steps, it's likely that you'll be energized and that you'll begin to see how God is accomplishing his vision through you.

But what happens if, after trying time after time, you're not able to complete the action steps.

Two possibilities emerge. One, the vision is not from God. In which case you'll need to return to the beginning steps of this process until you are certain of God's vision.

But the other possibility is that you are a Designer who needs a Developer.

Let me explain. In his *"Team Profile,"*[1] Bobb Biehl in chapter 7 has identified two leadership roles that must be understood at this stage of the vision process. Some leaders are Designers. "Designing" — conceiving the vision and the plan — energizes them. But they are not as interested or motivated or able to implement the plan.

Other leaders are Developers. While they may struggle with conceiving the vision, they love implementing it. Taking the action steps to accomplish a goal energizes them.

Some leaders are a combination of the two. They are Design/Developers. They take pleasure in designing the vision and the plan. But they also receive satisfaction from taking the necessary actions to see the dream come true.

Maybe you are a Designer who needs a Developer to help realize the vision. Or maybe you're a Developer with good implementation skills, but you need a Designer to clearly state the vision and plan.

If you have a vision, you are going to need the help of other people. You can't do everything yourself. If you do try to do everything yourself, you will end up with a small result. The bigger the vision, the more you need to recruit other people to your team. Recruit, equip, delegate, and release them into their part of the vision.

What Do You Need To Stop Doing?

After working for a time, you will find that there are jobs you and your team are doing that are not contributing to your vision.

For example, in our mission at Dynamic Church Planting International, one of our primary ministries was the assessment of church planting couples. We did a comprehensive and compassionate evaluation of a couple to determine their giftedness and calling for church planting. This process took a minimum of six weeks per assessment and, because of extensive referencing and psychological testing, was time consuming for DCPI's staff.

When the final assessment interview took place, several staff members would usually invest several hours.

So I looked at our vision: "Equipping leaders, churches and associations to impact the planting of one million dynamic churches to reach the world for Christ."

I knew that assessment of church planting leaders is important. Assessment is a service to potential church planting couples and church associations or denominations that wish to appoint them. A positive assessment greatly increases the probability that a couple will be successful in establishing a dynamic, new church.

But I could also see that each assessment required a significant amount of time and energy for our staff. And while assessment equips one couple, it wasn't by nature reproductive – the couple was not being equipped to assess others. So I asked myself: Can we impact the planting of a million dynamic churches by assessing one couple at a time? The answer was "No."

So, I went to our Executive Team and said: "Assessing couples for church planting is a very valuable ministry, and we have been doing it for years. However, each assessment takes a great deal of staff time and energy. It is not reproductive ministry. And, most importantly, it does not help us fulfill our vision to the degree that we need it to."

We stopped doing assessments. Because we believe in assessment, we networked leaders to other sources for this ministry.

The result of this decision was to free up staff energy and time for other ministries that helped us to fulfill our vision.

So what are you doing that is not helping you to get to your vision. What are you doing that is taking time, energy and money but does not fulfill your vision to the degree that is needed? Ask God to reveal his wisdom and discernment to you. Look at your vision statement. Look at your ministries. In what ways does each ministry reflect your vision? In what ways does each ministry fail to get you to your vision? And then ask, what do we need to stop doing?

This is a good exercise to go through at least once a year.

Such an exercise will save time, energy, and money that can be invested in other ministries that do help you realize the vision. It will say to your staff, "We can make the mid-course corrections that we need to make in order to stay in line with our vision." You and your staff members may experience an almost audible sigh of relief when you stop doing an activity that you need to stop.

What New Ministry Is The Lord Motivating You To Start?

And, perhaps most importantly, when you stop doing an activity this gives you time, energy and money to invest in a new activity that does reflect your vision.

What new ministry or program is the Lord encouraging you to start that is in line with your vision?

For example, the same year that we stopped doing assessments, DCPI started two new ministries: Dynamic Associates and Certified Trainers.2

Dynamic Associates are visionary church planting leaders who partner with us around the world to bring DCPI training to their nations. Certified Trainers are gifted teachers whom DCPI trains and certifies to teach our church planting courses around the world.

What we discovered is that both of these ministries have far greater potential to fulfill DCPI's vision than assessments would ever have done.

What new initiative or service is the Lord encouraging you to start that is in line with your vision? I would recommend that this question be the subject of a two or three day prayer retreat for you.

Work your plan. Stop doing what is not contributing to your vision. Start doing what will help you see your vision come true!

Strategically Plan the Vision Annually

Each year, make a major evaluation and update of your strategic plan.

For us, at DCPI, our process looks like this:

 **JULY**

First, the President takes a personal three-day retreat during July to pray and plan for the future. He considers the Vision and prays and thinks with the end in mind. What will the Vision look like when it is fulfilled? What steps do we need to take year after year in order to get to the outcome?

Like a normal prayer retreat, the President prays to hear from God, repents of his sins, pours over the Scripture, listens for God's instructions, and writes down the action steps and goals that will need to be communicated and delegated.

But the Strategic Planning Retreat is different from a regular prayer retreat because it emphasizes the Masterplanning process as described by Bobb Biehl (see chapter 7). Mr. Biehl emphasizes the creation of a Masterplanning Arrow3, which is both a process and a paradigm for envisioning your ministry.

I recommend you use Bobb Biehl's Masterplanning Arrow, as I do. Or you may prefer to us another comprehensive planning tool. Now use the Vision and your

Strategically plan your mission for the coming year. Look carefully at each element among the following elements in constructing your Master Plan:

 **Step 1.** What are the needs of your target population…the people you are called to serve. Any changes from when you put your initial plan together?

Step 2. What is your purpose as a mission? Here I would include your vision statement and your purpose statement. Any alterations needed here? This is less likely to change from year to year.

Step 3. What are your departments of ministry? Still the same? Or do you need to delete one department or put its function under another department? Or do you need to add a department?

Step 4. What are the milestones that have been achieved in the last year? Write them in your plan. Thank God for your milestones.

Step 5. What are the ideas that you and your staff have for the future? Write them down.

Step 6. What are the roadblocks that are keeping you from accomplishing your vision and mission? Record them. Be brutally honest with yourself.

Step 7. What resources do you have that will help you overcome your roadblocks? The top two resources we have at DCPI are these:

A. **Our God is our greatest resource.** Our Heavenly Father who wants to meet our needs, who will listen to our prayers and answer them.

B. **Our people are committed to the vision and mission of DCPI.** Our people include our Staff, Board, Spouses, DA's, CT's, Volunteers, Donors, Church Leaders and Foundation Executives.

Now it is time to look at your goals or priorities. As you look ahead, and according to your departments, what are your:

Long Range Priorities (6-50 years)

Mid-Range Priorities (3-5 years)

Short Range Priorities (0-2 years)

Quarterly Priorities (90 days)

Write it all down in your computer or in a notebook.

 **AUGUST**
Hold a three-day Executive Team Strategic Planning Retreat.

This would include your top leaders in each department of ministry. At DCPI this means our Vice Presidents and President. For you it may mean the Director of each department. This is the inner circle of your best leaders, thinkers, planners and pray-ers.

Include times of prayer, singing and devotion using the Word of God. (See an example of an Executive Team Strategic Planning Retreat Schedule in the appendix). Be creative. Meet the needs of your top leaders during this time.

Focus the best part of each day on your MasterPlan. Share with the Executive Team your thoughts about each step. Get them involved in good discussion. Ask them to give their best to accomplish the vision. I have often found that my Executive Team members have better ideas than I have. Often, you as a group will choose one of their ideas over one that came from your Personal Prayer and Planning Retreat. Listen especially to these top team members when they are talking about their own department and their goals for the coming year.

For each step on your Masterplan, you want your Executive Team to be unified concerning the direction and organization of your mission for the future. You want to come away from this Planning Retreat unified as a team regarding the goals that you are going to aim at for next year and beyond.

Invest some quality time at the end by working together to answer this question: What will our budget be for next year?

Or you may want to do what we do at DCPI. We learned from Dr. Steve Steele of the Maclellan Foundation to prepare three budgets for the year.

> #1 Necessary Budget: This budget is your basic, realistic budget. It is probably the same amount that you raised last year, if last year was a normal year. It doesn't include anything special—just what you need to keep the ministry running and alive for another year.

> #2. Growth Budget: This budget assumes a reasonable amount of growth in the ministry. Aim to bring in more money than last year and include some special projects.

> #3. Visionary Budget: This budget is what it would take to accomplish maximum productivity in your mission or ministry next year. It includes many special projects.

As a fundraiser, you will want to raise the Necessary Budget first, and then the Growth Budget. And then, if possible, you will want to raise the Visionary Budget. During a good year, you will raise your Growth Budget and perhaps some of your Visionary Budget.

But you are not done with working your plan yet.

SEPTEMBER

Now that you have your Executive Team in unity concerning the direction and budget for the upcoming year, it is time to have a Board Meeting.

Your Board Members are the leaders in the organization who are responsible before God for the ministry or mission. They should be mature, spiritual Christians who are top leaders in other ministries, missions or businesses. As the President or Senior Executive, you are accountable to them.

During a Board Meeting in September, you should bring out your Masterplanning Arrow. Ours at DCPI is seven feet long and four feet high, shaped like an arrow. It includes all the categories on it for every department of the mission. I discuss each category with our Board, take questions, and we make changes as needed. At the end of about a two-hour process of adjusting the MasterPlan, we are ready for a vote to affirm the DCPI Masterplanning Arrow for the following year.

This is a great time to present the budget, or your three budgets if that is the method you choose. Again, ask your Board for questions, make changes, and then ask for a vote of affirmation for next year's budget.

If you do this, you will have your next year's direction and your next year's budget approved by your Executive Staff and your Board of Directors three months in advance of that year.

You will be ready to raise money during the last three months of this year for next year's budget.

Your Executive Team will probably start working on next year's goals during the last three months of this year. This gives them a wonderful head start.

You will have a clear direction and know what it is going to cost to continue to see your vision come true.

Manage by objective.
As the directional leader of your mission or ministry, your primary task is to help your top staff leaders know their goals and work to accomplish objectives according to the MasterPlan. You will want to meet with your top department leaders one-to-one concerning their annual goals and objectives.

Help them to break down their goals and objectives by each quarter of the year. What goals and objectives are they planning to accomplish during the first three months (first quarter) of the year? Meet with them. Help them to accomplish their first quarter goals. Hold them accountable. Continue to meet with them on a regular basis throughout the year and keep them focused on their goals and objectives.

It is incredibly gratifying to see God's vision coming to pass in your ministry. Work your plan. Stop work that is not helping you to fulfill the vision. Start work that will help you to see the vision come true. Invest time, energy and money in your strategic planning. Facilitate the work of your Executive Team and your Board so that together you can effectively work your plan.

[1] Available through www.masterplanning.tv.

[2] For a description of these two ministries, see the Appendix.

[3] Masterplanning describes the use of the Arrow, and you can order the Arrow separately as well. Both are available through the website: www.masterplanning.tv.

Persevere in the Vision

Hebrews 11 is called the Heroes of the Faith chapter in the Bible. It could also be called the Visionary Heroes chapter. Hebrews 11 is a snapshot of some of the Bible's great visionaries and how their lives of faith and perseverance glorified God.

> [6] And without faith it is impossible to please God, because anyone who comes to him must believe that he exists and that he rewards those who earnestly seek him.

> [7] By faith Noah, when warned about things not yet seen, in holy fear built an ark to save his family. By his faith he condemned the world and became heir of the righteousness that comes by faith.

> [8] By faith Abraham, when called to go to a place he would later receive as his inheritance, obeyed and went, even though he did not know where he was going. [9] By faith he made his home in the promised land like a stranger in a foreign country; he lived in tents, as did Isaac and Jacob, who were heirs with him of the same promise. [10] For he was looking forward to the city with foundations, whose architect and builder is God.

> [11] By faith Abraham, even though he was past age—and Sarah herself was barren—was enabled to become a father because he considered him faithful who had made the promise. [12] And so from this one man, and he as good as dead, came descendants as numerous as the stars in the sky and as countless as the sand on the seashore.

¹³ All these people were still living by faith when they died. They did not receive the things promised; they only saw them and welcomed them from a distance. And they admitted that they were aliens and strangers on earth. (Heb. 11:6-13).

All of these people were living their faith…living out the vision that God had given them when they died. They didn't receive the fulfillment of the vision in their lifetimes, but they believed God and persevered in the vision.

²⁴ By faith Moses, when he had grown up, refused to be known as the son of Pharaoh's daughter. ²⁵ He chose to be mistreated along with the people of God rather than to enjoy the pleasures of sin for a short time. ²⁶ He regarded disgrace for the sake of Christ as of greater value than the treasures of Egypt, because he was looking ahead to his reward. ²⁷ By faith he left Egypt, not fearing the king's anger; he persevered because he saw him who is invisible. ²⁸ By faith he kept the Passover and the sprinkling of blood, so that the destroyer of the firstborn would not touch the firstborn of Israel (Heb. 11:24-28).

Moses could have lived in luxury as an Egyptian prince, but instead he chose the hardship of living with God's people. God gave him a vision: to lead his people out of Egyptian captivity and into the Land of Promise. And God also gave him a vision of his reward. So he persevered because he had experienced God in the burning bush (cf. Exodus 3).

²⁹ By faith the people passed through the Red Sea as on dry land; but when the Egyptians tried to do so, they were drowned.

³⁰ By faith the walls of Jericho fell, after the people had marched around them for seven days.

³¹ By faith the prostitute Rahab, because she welcomed the spies, was not killed with those who were disobedient.

³² And what more shall I say? I do not have time to tell about Gideon, Barak, Samson, Jephthah, David, Samuel and the prophets, ³³ who through faith conquered kingdoms, administered justice, and gained what was promised; who shut the mouths of lions, ³⁴ quenched the fury of the flames, and escaped the edge of the sword; whose weakness was turned to

strength; and who became powerful in battle and routed foreign armies (Heb. 11:29-32).

The Visionaries were indeed heroes. Look at all they accomplished in their one and only lives because they believed God and followed his vision for their lives. But they had to pay a price for that commitment.

> [35] Women received back their dead, raised to life again. Others were tortured and refused to be released, so that they might gain a better resurrection. [36] Some faced jeers and flogging, while still others were chained and put in prison. [37] They were stoned; they were sawed in two; they were put to death by the sword. They went about in sheepskins and goatskins, destitute, persecuted and mistreated— [38] the world was not worthy of them. They wandered in deserts and mountains, and in caves and holes in the ground. [39] These were all commended for their faith, yet none of them received what had been promised (Heb. 11:35-39).

The world was not worthy of these men and women...these visionary heroes...these heroes of the faith. They heard from God and did what he wanted them to do even when they were mistreated, persecuted, and put to death as a result. Again, the Word of God says that none of them received what had been promised. They didn't see their visions come true in their lifetimes.

What vision does God want to entrust to you that is so BIG that it can't be accomplished in your lifetime? So BIG that only God can accomplish this vision through generations of leaders. What is it?

Dr. Bill Bright, the founder and long time leader of Campus Crusade, had a vision of planting five million churches in the latter years of his life. He has passed from this life into the arms of Jesus. After he died, leaders that loved Bill Bright hosted a series of Church Planting Congresses to complete the vision of five million churches planted.

Persevere through your time of testing.

The Lord entrusted me with the Vision of a Million Churches in June of 1997. Yet, during the years 2001 through 2003, I wondered if I should continue as the President of Dynamic Church Planting International.

What happened? My testing came on several fronts. My first wife, Jule, died in 1999 after a nine-year breast cancer battle. The cancer battle was exhausting and terrible. When she graduated to heaven, I became the single father of two teenagers. It was very difficult to go through these years of loss and personal responsibility as a single dad while trying to keep our mission moving in the right direction. I wondered if DCPI would be better served by a leader who could offer more energy to the mission than I had available.

The Lord provided a great gift to me by the name of Cathy Cooper. She began as a prayer partner and encourager for me. Because of her church planting, mentoring, and marketing experience, she joined our staff in January of 2000 and became my mission partner. Love blossomed and she became my wife on May 6, 2000.

There were staff members in our mission who could not adapt to the fact that DCPI was changing and left the mission. That was painful for everyone on the team and made me question my leadership.

We entered into an agreement to lease more and better office space in 1999 and incurred a significant monthly payment as a result. Shortly after that, the United States economy moved into a recession that lasted from 2000 to 2003. As a result, many donors stopped or drastically reduced their giving. Churches and parachurch ministries in the United States were hurting financially. DCPI was no exception. Our total income for 2003 was only about 50% of what it had been in 1999.

As the President, I believed it was my responsibility to raise money for the mission. But there were many more closed doors than open doors for fundraising from 2000 to 2003. I felt like a fundraising failure.

We cut costs. Cathy negotiated with the landlord to return one-third of our leased space and that significantly lowered our monthly expense. We cut costs again, eliminating everything that wasn't absolutely needed to stay alive as a mission.

One of my most difficult decisions was to stop providing funding for one of our DCPI staff. He was one of my best friends and the first person I recruited for DCPI when the mission began in 1994. Like me and all our staff, he was a faith-supported missionary. But in 1995 DCPI also began supplying a portion of his monthly salary to compensate him for administrative work.

Because DCPI's monthly deficit continued to grow, I had to tell this dear brother that we could no longer support him. Soon after, he transitioned to another mission. Within two years, he contracted cancer and passed away. We remained close friends until the day he died, but it was very painful to see him leave our mission.

Financially, God provided just what we absolutely needed to keep the doors open at DCPI.

I was tired, grieving, and felt like a failure in fund raising and in leading our staff. I confided in Cathy and in my personal mentor, Dr. Charlie Bradshaw, that I wondered whether I was the right person to continue to lead our mission.

Both of them were affirming and encouraging. They helped me to keep on keeping on. They reminded me that God was working dramatically to fulfill his vision for our mission in the midst of a season of trial.

It was in 2000 at Billy Graham's Amsterdam 2000, that God gave us 1004 leaders from 72 nations who signed up for our church planting training. That was 10 times as many leaders as we hoped to connect with in Amsterdam.

They reminded me that we trained 801 church planters in 2003. That exceeded the number we trained in 1999 and God did this through us in 2003 on only half the budget of 1999.

They pointed out that we had published a new Handbook for church planters – The New Dynamic Church Planting Handbook, based on 12 biblical principles of church planting. In addition to our national training, they pointed out that in 2003 DCPI trained in Ghana, India, Italy, the Ivory Coast, Kenya, Malawi, Nepal, the Netherlands and Uganda.

We brought on three Executive Staff members. We began training trainers for our "church planting essentials" and called them Certified Trainers. We began to recruit leaders of church planting movements who had a vision to impact the planting of at least 100 churches in their lifetimes. We called them Dynamic Associates.

Rev. Emmanuel Donkoh of Ghana, Africa, and Rev. Jayakumar of India become our first Dynamic Associates certified as basic trainers. The First Annual Dynamic Associate Summit was held in June 2003. DCPI equipped Certified Trainers and Dynamic Associates from seven nations and six US states.

Yes, the years from 1999 to 2003 was a season of testing. But God kept fulfilling his Vision for our Mission during those years, too. And, as Cathy and Charlie encouraged me, the Lord kept using and blessing my leadership as well.

So what should you do? Persevere in the Vision that God has given.

How many great visions from God have been sacrificed because the leader to whom God gave the vision quit? We have a saying: when the going gets tough, the tough get going.

Here are Bible passages that, if you plant them in your heart, will help you to persevere. The phrases in bold are emphasized by me.

I was tired, grieving, and felt like a failure

[32] Remember those earlier days after you had received the light, when you stood your ground in a great contest in the face of suffering. [33] Sometimes you were publicly exposed to insult and persecution; at other times you stood side by side with those who were so treated. [34] You sympathized with those in prison and joyfully accepted the confiscation of your property, because you knew that you yourselves had better and lasting possessions. [35] So do not throw away your confidence; it will be richly rewarded. [36] You need to persevere so that when you have done the will of God, you will receive what he has promised. [37] For in just a very little while, "He who is coming will come and will not delay. [38] But my righteous one will live by faith. And if he shrinks back, I will not be pleased with him." [39] But we are not of those who shrink back and are destroyed, but of those who believe and are saved (Heb. 10:32-39).

Persevere in the vision. Do not shrink back. Have faith in the Lord and in the vision.

[3] Not only so, but we also rejoice in our sufferings, because we know that **suffering produces perseverance;** [4] **perseverance, character;** and character, hope. [5] And hope does not disappoint us, because God has poured out his love into our hearts by the Holy Spirit, whom he has given us (Rom. 5:3-5).

Suffering builds our capacity to persevere. And the Lord uses that perseverance to strengthen our characters, so we'll become more mature leaders. The result is we're better able to be stewards of the vision he has entrusted to us.

Therefore, since we are surrounded by such a great cloud of witnesses, let us throw off everything that hinders and the sin that so easily entangles, and let us run with perseverance the race marked out for us (Heb. 12:1).

What is the race marked out for you? What is God's vision for you? Run that race and run it with resolve and determination.

> ² Let us fix our eyes on Jesus, the author and perfecter of our faith, who for the joy set before him endured the cross, scorning its shame, and sat down at the right hand of the throne of God. ³ **Consider him who endured such opposition from sinful men, so that you will not grow weary and lose heart** (Heb. 12:2-3).

Everyone gets tired. Don't make any big decisions when you are tired. Rest, recuperate, and then spend an extended time with God. Make those big decisions when your heart is full of His presence.

> ² Consider it pure joy, my brothers, whenever you face trials of many kinds, 3 because you know that **the testing of your faith develops perseverance. 4 Perseverance must finish its work so that you may be mature and complete, not lacking anything** (James 1:2-4).

Remember, God has entrusted a vision into your care. He is as concerned about you…and your maturity…as he is with completing the vision. God wants to build you into a complete leader, not lacking anything. And that can only come about when your faith, your vision, is tested. My pastor mentor, Dr. Penny Penhollow, told me: "It isn't the easy times that make a person—it is the hard times that make a person." How true that is! Getting tested is not easy. But we can rejoice in our times of testing because God is using them to make us more complete Christians and leaders, better able to be the steward for the vision he has entrusted us with.

Pray for God's Favor for the Vision

Consider Galatians 6:9: "Let us not become weary in doing good, for at the proper time we will reap a harvest if we do not give up."

If you persevere through a season of testing, the Lord often blesses the vision and your ministry with a season of favor. Yes, you will reap a harvest if you don't give up. That is just what happened at Dynamic Church Planting International beginning in 2004.

DCPI received the first in a series of foundation grants. This really helped to bring health to our finances. Forty-one leaders of church planting movements from eleven nations attended the Second Annual Dynamic Associate Summit Week. More crucial staff members joined the team. Together, our staff and Certified Trainers equipped 1964 church planting leaders. This training took place in 9 nations: Colombia, Democratic Republic of the Congo, Ethiopia, Ghana, India, Kenya, Liberia, Tanzania and the USA. In 2005, God empowered our staff and Certified Trainers to train more than 4000 leaders from 16 nations. Praise God for his favor!

If your ministry is a ship on the open sea, your vision is the rudder. It keeps you pointed in the right direction toward the right destination.

Do not persevere in a ministry longer than the Lord desires.

This is the counterpoint to persevering in the vision. It is very possible to stay longer in a project than God wants you to. For example, after two and a half years in my first church plant, I no longer had a vision for what God wanted me to do.

When I prayed for vision, all I saw was darkness. I had no leading from him beyond three years. Though I tried to persevere, I can see now that the Lord wanted me to transition out of that church. No vision after three years was his sign that I should leave and follow him into my next ministry.

It is my experience that many Christian leaders stay in a ministry longer than they should, longer than the Lord wants them to. Often they persevere because as Christians we value perseverance. Sometimes it may be because they don't know what to do next. Or maybe they stay because their ministry represents financial security.

It is not easy to determine if you are to persevere in the vision or leave the ministry because God is re-directing you. These major decisions should be the subject of personal prayer retreats and the wise counsel of other leaders who have a genuine love and concern for the servant of God who is at a point of ministry decision.

Find your successor.

Whether you are in a time of testing or a time of favor, it is crucial that you find and mentor potential leaders to succeed you in your role in your church, ministry or mission. Who will take over for you when you are gone? Ask God to give you leaders whom you can mentor who have the right characteristics to succeed you. Put a succession plan in place that will help your Board know what to do and who to turn to when you are no longer able to serve in your role.

10

Vision and the Kingdom of God

In August of 2000, five members of the DCPI staff traveled to the Netherlands for Amsterdam 2000. Our Lord, through Billy Graham and his team, gathered the largest group of evangelists in the history of the world. More than 11,000 of us were present. DCPI had a booth there and our goal was to begin a relationship with 100 evangelists who had a heart for church planting. We felt led to offer free church planting training to those who would qualify by filling out an application form and going through a brief interview.

The booth opened and the flood of leaders came. After the first three hours, we were amazed that more than 100 leaders had already signed up for training. By the end of Amsterdam 2000, 1004 leaders from 72 nations had signed up for DCPI training. We were overwhelmed with gratitude to God for showering us with leaders. Through Amsterdam 2000, the Lord took a big step toward fulfilling his vision of a million dynamic churches.

One of the questions on the application form was: "If we provide you with free training, what will you do with it when you return to your country?" We noticed that, time and again, the African leaders would answer with something like this: "I will take the training that you provide and I will go home to my country. There I will train my ten or twenty friends in ministry. Together, we will go out and plant churches."

We began to realize we were hearing a "Kingdom-mindset." These leaders cared about expanding the Kingdom of God, and seemed even more concerned about evangelism and church planting throughout their country than with their individual churches.

We were also hearing a reproductive mindset. These African leaders were expressing the very essence of 2 Timothy 2:2 "And the things you have heard me say in the presence of many witnesses entrust to reliable men who will also be qualified to teach others."

We began to reflect upon our ministry in the United States. Often US leaders would come to us to help them plant one church. Rarely did they think of equipping others so that multiple churches would be planted and the Kingdom advanced. They frequently cited the great cost in starting a new church as the reason for focusing only on their own congregation.

The American leaders had far more money and other resources than the Africans. Yet the Africans seemed to be focused on expanding God's kingdom — on reproducing their training and planting multiple churches. They were trusting God to provide for each leader and each church.

Look at and listen to Jesus:

> At daybreak Jesus went out to a solitary place. The people were looking for him and when they came to where he was, they tried to keep him from leaving them. But he said, "I must preach the good news of the kingdom of God to the other towns also, because that is why I was sent" (Luke 4:42-43).

If Jesus was concerned with just that one group of people, he would have stayed in that one town. But he kept moving. He had a "Kingdom-mindset." The very reason he was sent into the world was to spread the good news to many towns.

Jesus taught us to love the Kingdom of God and to be committed to expanding it. The phrase "kingdom of God" is found 54 times in the Gospels. The phrase "kingdom of heaven" is found 32 times in Matthew alone. Obviously our Lord wants us to be concerned with more than the one church to which we belong. Though he wants us to be committed to our church, he calls us to spread the Kingdom of God throughout our world.

North American Christians have some great advantages, like thorough theological training and abundant resources. But often we do not have a "Kingdom-mindset." I believe this is one of the main reasons why North America is not experiencing the rapid growth of the Kingdom of God yet.

49% of the world's population live in nations that are experiencing the rapid growth of the Kingdom of God according to Jim Montgomery, the Founder of DAWN. (Discipling a Whole Nation). My experience is that most of the Christian leaders in these nations have a pervasive Kingdom mindset. They want to see the rule of King Jesus here, there and everywhere throughout the world.

What does this have to do with vision? Your vision needs to look beyond your church. Many Christian leaders think too small. They are consumed with thoughts about "our church," as if it was the only church, a little kingdom all by itself. Sadly, what happens beyond "their church" is of little concern to them.

That wasn't true for Jesus. And it shouldn't be true for you.

See your vision as a part of what God is doing as he brings about his Kingdom rule throughout the world.

What is the Kingdom of God? The Kingdom of God is the rule of God, and all the blessings and advantages that flow from his rule in our lives. In the Bible, The Kingdom of God is past, present and future. In our day, The Kingdom of God includes all true Christians gathered in churches all around the world.

If our goal is to become like Jesus, we must open our minds and hearts to what God is doing in his Kingdom around the world. Pray that God will give you a vision that is part of his vision to extend his kingdom around the world.

His wonderful, all-powerful rule is gaining momentum in many countries around the world. The Kingdom of God is coming quickly in India, and China, and Africa and South America. Yes, the Kingdom of God is coming! What should YOU do about that?

Here are some facts about how quickly God's Kingdom in coming!

Mission Frontiers is the bulletin of the U.S. Center for World Mission. In an article titled 'The State of World Evangelization'

www.missionfrontiers.org/newslinks/statewe.htm), you will find these approximate 2000 Global Mission Statistics:

" In 1974 approximately one half of the world's population was beyond the reach of the Church, living in unreached people groups. Today, just one third of the world's population live in unreached peoples beyond the reach of the Church."

" As the figures below demonstrate, we are in the final era of missions. For the first time in history we can anticipate the completion of the missionary task, which is to establish an indigenous church planting movement within the language and social structure of every people on earth."

" Overall World Population is growing by 1.6% each year

Pentecostals and Charismatics 7.3%

Evangelicals 5.7%,

Protestants 2.9%,

Roman Catholics ~1.2%,

Muslims 2.7%

Evangelical believers are growing at a rate of three and one half times that of world population."

Why is God accelerating the growth of His Kingdom around the world? I believe it is the fulfillment of this prophecy: Jesus said, in Matthew 24: 14, "And this gospel of the kingdom will be preached in the whole world as a testimony to all nations, and then the end will come."

Our God is extending his kingdom rule all over the world! For us Christians it is the most exciting time in history to be alive! Get in on it. Don't let it pass you by.

All of the King's subjects have a role to play as King Jesus extends His rule. What does God want you to do? Are you to pray? Are you to go? Are you to give? What is your role?

In light of this new information, what is God's vision for your life and ministry?

What should you do?

At Dynamic Church Planting International, we want to see people all over the world come to Christ. We believe that the church is God's instrument for evangelizing the world. And we believe that planting new churches is the best way to reach the most people for Christ around the globe. We have a vision of one million new churches reaching people for Christ in every nation. Our job at DCPI is to train the leaders who will plant these dynamic churches worldwide.

In November of 2003, I was a member of our DCPI Training Team in Ghana, West Africa. The Lord enabled us to train 120 leaders in how to plant churches in

Ghana. And while that it was exciting, it was not the most thrilling part of the story. We also certified seven Ghanaian leaders as Trainers in DCPI's basic church planting track. Each of them invested the entire first week in being trained. Then, under the DCPI Team's supervision, they traveled to a second city to train other leaders. In the future, these Certified Trainers will help our top Ghana leader, Rev. Emmanuel Donkoh, train hundreds of church planters in Ghana and throughout Africa.

We also recruited six Ghanaian leaders as Dynamic Associates. A Dynamic Associate is a leader of a church planting movement. These six will help Rev. Donkoh expand church planting movements in Ghana and in other countries in Africa.

The result of this equipping will be hundreds of new churches established in Ghana and other African nations. These churches will reach tens of thousands of precious people for Christ.

The Kingdom of God is coming quickly in Ghana.

Let me challenge you to do a personal study of the "Kingdom of God" in the Gospels. Your thinking will be transformed and your priorities will change. You will love your church, but you will see that there is so much more that Jesus wants for you — the Kingdom of God.

After all, Jesus taught frequently about the Kingdom of God.

Here's how Matthew described the beginning of Jesus' ministry in Galilee:

> Jesus went throughout Galilee, teaching in their synagogues, **preaching the good news of the kingdom**, and healing every disease and sickness among the people (Mt. 4:23, my emphasis).

The same theme dominated his teaching three years later, after the resurrection:

After his suffering, he showed himself to these men and gave many convincing proofs that he was alive. He appeared to them over a period of forty days and **spoke about the kingdom of God** (Acts 1:3, my emphasis).

From beginning to end, Jesus spoke about the Kingdom of God.

And notice how the book of Acts described the ministry of the Apostle Paul. This verse summarizes the Apostle Paul's ministry: Boldly and without hindrance **he preached the kingdom of God and taught about the Lord Jesus Christ** (Acts 28:31, my emphasis).

Don't live for a small vision! Don't create an "our church" vision! Live for a Kingdom vision!

When Jesus taught about the Kingdom, he used the analogy of the harvest.

> **" The one who sowed the good seed is the Son of Man. The field is the world, and the good seed stands for the sons of the kingdom. The weeds are the sons of the evil one, and the enemy who sows them is the devil. The harvest is the end of the age, and the harvesters are angels** (Mt. 13:37-39).

The harvest around the world is ripening and one day soon it will be gathered in. Both the wheat and the weeds, those who are Christians, and those who are not, will be exposed. And then it will be too late for those who don't know Jesus.

> **" As the weeds are pulled up and burned in the fire, so it will be at the end of the age"** (Mt. 13:40).

At the end of the age, those who have not accepted Christ as Lord and Savior will be without hope. Like Satan, they will be pulled up and cast into everlasting fire. King Jesus is coming—that is the urgency! The last chance to come to Christ and his Kingdom is just around the corner.

> **The Son of Man will send out his angels, and they will weed out of his kingdom everything that causes sin and all who do evil. They will throw them into the fiery furnace, where there will be weeping and gnashing of teeth** (Mt. 13:41-42).

Of course there will be weeping and hopeless grieving as people realize their chance to enter heaven is over. If they have not received King Jesus, they will be cast into the fiery furnace.

> **Then the righteous will shine like the sun in the kingdom of their Father. He who has ears, let him hear** (Mt. 13:43).

Those who have received Jesus as their King will be brought into the Kingdom of Heaven—the Kingdom of Light. Christians will shine with a righteousness not their own—it is the righteousness of the Savior, King Jesus. They will shine like the Son, reflecting the glory of God himself.

Friends, if Jesus is sitting on that throne in your heart, you are a subject of the Kingdom of God. If Jesus is your King, what will you do? What will you do with your time? What will you do with your energy? What will you do with your money? Do your part to spread the rule of King Jesus around the world!

1. **Passionately pray the Lord's Prayer.** "Our Father in heaven, hallowed be your name, your kingdom come, your will be done on earth as it is in heaven (Mt. 6:9-10, emphasis added). Pray for the Kingdom to come. It is coming!

2. **Go and spread the good news!** Tell people about Jesus in your neighborhood and community. Help your church reach out to the lost people in your village, town, or city.

3. **Reach the world for Christ** by planting churches that will plant churches.

Let God expand your vision from your church or mission to the world! The best way to reach the most people is by planting dynamic, reproductive churches in every neighborhood and village, in every language and cultural group around the globe. What part will you play in God's great vision?

If you need training for church planting, get it. (Contact DCPI and we'll do our best to help you. www.dcpi.org.) But don't focus on only one church. Focus on expanding the Kingdom through multiplying dynamic new churches. Help us train church planters. That is the way we can reach every nation for Christ!

Don't be afraid. Be bold. Be strong. Be blessed.

See your Vision come true!

How can I become
a DCPI Dynamic Associate or Certified Trainer?

Our DCPI Vision is to: Equip leaders, churches and associations to impact the planting of one million dynamic churches to reach the world for Christ.

Is God stirring in your heart to help make this **Million Church Vision** a reality? Are you a gifted teacher or leader? Are you interested in becoming a volunteer with DCPI? If so, you may want to apply to become a DCPI Dynamic Associate or a Certified Trainer. These are non-paid positions.

By 2020, we believe that there will be 5000 Dynamic Associates and Certified Trainers equipping leaders to plant vibrant churches worldwide in every nation. We call this team **The Fellowship of the 5000.**

We are looking for Christians who demonstrate spiritual maturity, servant leadership, and commitment to evangelism through church planting. These character traits and passion are true for both positions. In both cases we are looking for…

Spiritual Maturity

Exemplifies a Christ-like character according to the qualities of 1Timothy 3 and Titus 1.

Committed and connected to the local church

Committed to practice and teach God's Word.

In full agreement with DCPI's doctrinal statement

Dependent upon prayer

Caring, compassionate, approachable, humble.

Servant Leadership

Recognized and respected by other leaders who know him well

Experienced in church planting.

Reproduces his life and ministry.

Committed to equipping and mentoring other church planting leaders

Commitment to Evangelism through Church Planting

Deeply desires to reach lost people for Christ

Motivated to join in realizing DCPI's "Million Church Vision"

Creates opportunities for DCPI to train with him among his target population and in his target countries.

But what are the differences between these two DCPI roles?

A Certified Trainer is...

A gifted trainer and teacher.

Equipped by DCPI to train church planting leaders in a specific track of training.

A trainer whom DCPI endorses to carry our training to new networks of church planters.

Experienced in the kind of training that the track is communicating. (For example, we would expect the certified trainer to have experience in mentoring if he or she is training in the mentor track.)

A DCPI staff member, a denominational leader, a Dynamic Associate, or a friend.

A Dynamic Associate is a....

Visionary with a goal to impact the planting of at least 100 churches in his lifetime.

Leader who desires to join his vision to our DCPI Vision of a Million.

Leader of a church planting movement.

Leader who has regional or national influence among local church leaders.

Leader within his own organization, mission or church. Serving as a DCPI Dynamic Associate is his secondary ministry.

Not a DCPI staff member.

When you think Certified Trainer, think "Trainer/Teacher." When you think Dynamic Associate, think "Visionary Leader." You can be who you are at DCPI. If you are a gifted trainer/teacher, you can become a Certified Trainer. If you are a gifted visionary leader, you can become a Dynamic Associate. And if you are gifted in vision, leading and training, you can become BOTH a Dynamic Associate AND a Certified Trainer.

Our ultimate goal for the Certified Trainer: Certified to train in every track we offer at DCPI.

Our ultimate goal for the Dynamic Associate: Actively bringing DCPI training to new networks of church planting leaders.

You can see how the Certified Trainer can equip hundreds of church planting leaders over the course of a ministry career which will lead to the planting of thousands of new, dynamic churches. The Dynamic Associate, the visionary leader of a church planting movement in countries all over the world will provide opportunities for the training of hundreds of leaders who will establish thousands of churches.

If you are a teacher or a leader, you can apply to join The Fellowship of the 5000. This is a team of DCPI Certified Trainers and Dynamic Associates who are bringing effective, high-quality church planting training to the nations of the world.

To learn more about applying as a DCPI Certified Trainer or Dynamic Associate, go to DCPI's website: **www.dcpi.org**

Seeing Your Vision Come True

Worksheet

This is your tool to see your vision come true. We know that the vision, plan and timeline must come from God. Please pray through each of your responses to these questions and guiding statements. My prayer is the God will give you what you need to see his vision come true through you and your team.

Read Chapter 1 The Story of a Vision from God

How do you ask questions of the Lord and receive his answers?

How do you listen to God and receive His vision?

What need or needs does your vision meet?

What will the world look like when your vision is fulfilled?

What other leaders will need to give input to your vision statement?

Read Chapter 2 Whose Vision Is It Anyway?

What is your definition of a vision?

How will you make sure that your vision is a vision from God?

What are the benefits of a vision from God in contrast to a 'man-made' vision?

Do you believe that the Bible teaches that it is good to hear from the Holy Spirit and that the Holy Spirit wants to communicate with you?

Would you say that you are closed, open or highly motivated to hear from God and why?

Read Chapter 3 How to Receive a Vision from God

How do you feel about spending two or three days alone with God? What is the best place can you go to be alone and to hear from God?

Schedule your three day prayer and planning retreat. (Do not allow anything to stand in the way of going on your prayer retreat).

Follow the Twelve Steps to an Effective Prayer Retreat or personalize your plan from the steps and write down your response to each of the twelve steps.

Will you develop a spiritual discipline of taking at least two prayer retreats each year so that you can listen to your God and Father?

Read Chapter 4 How to Refine Your Vision

Are you committed to praying about your vision daily?

What are some ways you can best share the vision with the top influencers in your organization?

Who are the trusted and wise leaders who will help you shape the vision? Will you receive their wisdom and allow it to clarify the vision?

Boil your vision down into a concise, motivational vision statement. What is it?

Read Chapter 5 Communicate the Vision to the Right People

How will you get your top leaders, your Board, to adopt the vision?

What are the names of people you will you ask to pray for the vision? Do they have a gift for prayer?

How will you use your vision to recruit staff members? How will the vision benefit your staff?

How will your vision help your donors to invest in the mission? How will the vision benefit your staff?

Ask God to give you the names of people and organizations that he wants use to bring about the vision. What are the names that God is bringing to your mind? Who is God drawing to your vision?

(Are you interested in becoming a DCPI Dynamic Associate or Certified Trainer? Let us know at **service@dcpi.org** or go to our website at **www.dcpi.org** and apply)

Read Chapter 6 How to Communicate Your Vision

Write the story of your vision? How will you communicate your vision story?

What are some ways that you can communicate your vision? Which ways will you use?

How often do you plan to communicate your vision?

What is the symbol of your vision?

Have your staff members and key leaders memorize your vision statement.

Read Chapter 7. Use Your Vision to Plan Your Work

What do you believe about planning?

Write down your Strategic Plan by answering the questions in 'Creating Your Plan' in the Appendix.

How will you include your staff and board in your annual strategic planning?

Update your Strategic Plan each year.

Read Chapter 8. Use Your Vision to Work Your Plan

Do you need a designer or a developer? And who are potential leaders within your relationships that could serve as your designer or developer?

Look at your vision statement. What activities do you need to stop doing?

Look at your vision statement. What is the Lord leading you to start doing that will really help to fulfill the vision?

Annually, revise your Plan.

Create your annual budget.

How are you involving your Executive Staff and Board Members in the process of finalizing your MasterPlan and Budget for the year?

How are you managing your team by the objectives that are set?

Chapter 9 Persevere in the Vision

Who is your favorite visionary hero from the Bible and why? Who is your favorite contemporary visionary hero and why?

What are the challenges to your vision and mission that make you want to quit? How are you prepared to persevere through persecution and great discouragement to see your vision come true?

What Bible passage gives you the most encouragement to 'keep on keeping on'?

Who are your encouragers? Who are the people in your life that you count on to encourage you to persevere in your vision?

How are you praying for God to bless your ministry with favor?

Do you still have a vision for this ministry? Are you persevering longer than the Lord desires? What will you do in order to make the right, Godly decisions about your future and the future of the ministry?

There is no success without a successor. Write down your preliminary succession plan. How will you help your board and staff to work with you to complete your succession plan?

Chapter 10 Vision and the Kingdom of God

Do you have a reproductive, Kingdom mind-set? Describe your mind-set.

What did Jesus teach about the Kingdom of God?

How does your vision help to advance God's Kingdom?

What is your role in the expansion of God's Kingdom throughout the world?

Strategic Planning Tool

Answer these questions to complete your Vision-Plan-TimeLine.

VISION:

Prepare a written statement of your unique vision. (Describe in concrete terms what this idealized picture looks like).

Who are you trying to help?

What are their needs?

How will you meet their needs?

What values will your organization embrace?

What are your organization's name, logo, and slogan?

Describe the number and type of staff that your organization will require.

PLAN:
Describe your personal role in the vision.

What are your goals?
    Short term (90 days).

        Medium term (90 days to 2 years).

        Long Term (2 years to 50 years).

Describe the steps that you need to take in order to share the dream and gain ownership by the appropriate decision makers.

What objections to your vision do you anticipate? How will you answer them?

What roadblocks to implementing your vision and plan will you encounter? How will you overcome these roadblocks?

What resources will your organization need and where will you find them?

How will you recruit, assess and equip the staff?

How much will your vision cost? Formulate a first draft of a proposed budget (including startup expenses for the first year before birth).

What means will you pursue to financially support the staff and the project?

TIMELINE

Make a comprehensive list of the action steps you and your team need to take in order to accomplish each short term and medium term goal?

Place your tasks on your TimeLine.

Quarterly TimeLine

13 Weeks (Record actual dates)

CHURCH PLANTING ESSENTIALS — TaskList	4 Feb	11 Feb	18 Feb	25 Feb	4 Mar	11 Mar	18 Mar	25 Mar	1 Apr	8 Apr	15 Apr	22 Apr	29 Apr	
Pray and fast for God's vision	●													✓
Write out vision		●·····|												✓
Design a process of discipleship			●···········											✓
Find a mentor	●··												→
Recruit a leadership board	●··												→
Survey community — 500 doors	●···········												✓
Start one to one discipleship											●·····			✗
Study demographics in community	●·····													✓

Quarterly TimeLine

13 Weeks (Record actual dates)

PROJECT:

TaskList

At the end of
each quarter:
Done   ✓
Continue →
Begin   ✗

Page _____

94

Made in the USA
Lexington, KY
22 October 2012